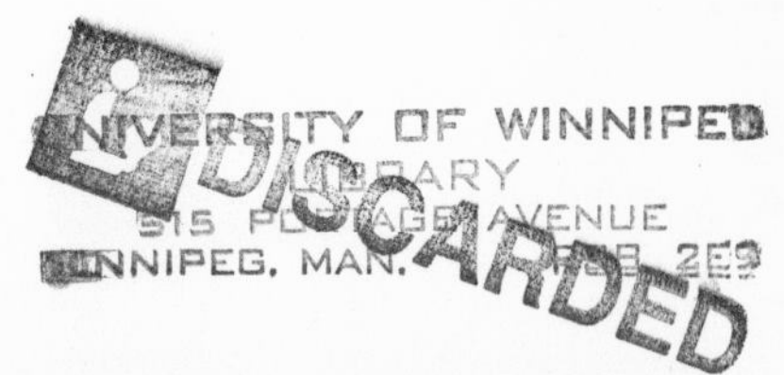
UNIVERSITY OF WINNIPEG
LIBRARY
515 PORTAGE AVENUE
WINNIPEG, MAN. R3B 2E9
DISCARDED

EMERSON'S THEORIES OF LITERARY EXPRESSION

BY

EMERSON GRANT SUTCLIFFE

Phaeton Press
New York
1971

Originally Published 1918
Reprinted 1971

Published by PHAETON PRESS, INC.
Library of Congress Catalog Card Number 73-131261
SBN 87753-049-1

PREFACE

This study is practically identical with the dissertation which I submitted at the University of Illinois in 1918 in partial fulfillment of the requirements for the doctorate in English.

In an embryonic state, it was looked over and kindly criticised by Professor Mervin James Curl and Professor Stuart Pratt Sherman. I am most grateful for the encouragement which they gave me to develop the subject more fully. To Professor Jacob Zeitlin, under whose direction the thesis was brought to completion, I am conscious of the highest obligations. His wise overseership, product of sound sense and catholic learning, heartened me to give of my best to the undertaking, and at the same time was never of so intrusive a character as to have offended the most sensitive believer in Emersonian self-reliance.

Though the matter is most personal, I cannot resist referring here to the genesis of the book. My sponsors in baptism, who gave me the name of Emerson, are of course initially responsible. And who shall measure the influence of the copy of *Representative Men*, given to me on my first Christmas by another name-father and another participant in the christening above-mentioned, the Rev. Percy Stickney Grant?

The extended extracts from the *Journals* and the *Works* in what follows are printed with the generous permission of Houghton Mifflin Company, the authorized publishers of Emerson's writings.

University of Minnesota,
August, 1922.

TABLE OF CONTENTS

EMERSON, TRANSCENDENTALISM, AND STYLISTIC THEORY

Controversy about Ralph Waldo Emerson's manner of expression has been warm and long-enduring; misconceptions regarding it have been rife; but little has been said about the principles of writing which he professed. Yet the connection between his beliefs and his performance is close and important. The notorious brokenness of his style is as much the result of set purpose as of incapacity. And on the other hand, the qualities for which his style is treasured—the pith and pungency of his epigrams, the mingled grandeur and homeliness of his metaphors—are also outgrowths of a considered philosophy of style. It is the aim of this book to show the connection between this philosophy of style and the Emersonian philosophy in general; and, more especially, to gather for lovers of Emerson and the art of writing some of the profuse but scattered wealth of his stimulating comment on literary expression.

The value of so doing will become more apparent through a review of what critics have said about the style itself. Not all have a right to Emerson's praise of Landor as a critic who has "examined before he has expatiated."[1] Critics of Emerson's style have been numberless; examiners, especially those who have subjected his manner of writing to careful, detailed analysis, few. Among those who have had their eye firmly fixed on the object itself there can hardly be reckoned the critics of greatest general reputation, Arnold[2] and Viscount Morley.[3] These men say much that is true of Emerson's incontinuity and structural weakness, but they point out the compensations for this defect most charily. This is perhaps to be expected of classicized litterateurs, who are temperamentally unfitted to appreciate either the homely or the transcendental. In criticism of style, sympathy must accompany, if indeed it does not produce, discernment.

Two treatments of Emerson's style seem to me peculiarly satisfactory, as combining both knowledge and understanding: those by John Burroughs[4] and Professor O. W. Firkins.[5] Burroughs is interested, like Emerson, in nature, poetry, and style, and is thoroughly at home in the Concord atmosphere. He regards Emerson's manner of expression as the best which

[1] *Natural History of Intellect: Papers from the Dial, Walter Savage Landor.*

[2] *Discourses in America: Emerson.*

[3] *Critical Miscellanies I: Emerson.*

[4] *Birds and Poets: Emerson.* See my note on Burroughs' Emersonian essay, *Expression,* in the bibliography at the end of this book.

[5] *Ralph Waldo Emerson.*

New England could produce: lacking in mass and unction, but electric in its epigrammatic brilliancy, sustained intellectuality, and power to inspire. Professor Firkins' treatment is unique in being based on definite and complete acquaintance with the *Journals*, the publication of which was completed in 1914. This knowledge of the *Journals* is important, for the revelations there have enabled him to criticise as one fully aware of what Emerson was actually striving for stylistically. In his minute but decidedly sane investigation, he has isolated and pinned down with admirable, though perhaps terrifying nicety, the specific qualities of the style.

Other writers—notably Garnett,[6] Holmes,[7] Lowell,[8] and Brownell[9]—have pointed out these characteristics, though none with such inclusiveness. It has been generally agreed that the style is compact and pointed rather than flowing, and memorable rather in sentences than in entire essays; that it has been influenced for better or for worse by the eloquence of Everett and Channing and the requirements of the lecture platform; that it is both surprising and felicitous in its use of the right word in the right place; that its tropes are extraordinary in their combination of apt adjustment and spiritual power; and that altogether it has on the reader a lifting, arousing, and ennobling effect.

Obviously, such a style deserves study. What, then, is to be said of the theories of literary expression which Emerson professed, and which, put into practice, resulted in this style? He has not concealed the secrets of his workshop. A remarkable proportion of the *Works* consists of his reflections and discoveries concerning the art and process of writing. There are two essays on *Eloquence*, one on *The Superlative*, one on *Art and Criticism*, one on *Inspiration*, one on *The Poet*, one on *Poetry and Imagination*, and there are scattered dicta in quantities on the same general subject. The *Journals* add at least as great a bulk of material.

"Why has never the poorest country college offered me a professorship of rhetoric?" asked Emerson in his journal in 1862.[10] For such a chair his equipment was certainly ideal. He could write, in the first place; and in the second place, he knew his subject thoroughly. From childhood he had practised the art and had been concerned about means for perfecting himself in it. "It was as natural to this boy to write as to another to play ball," says Dr. Edward Emerson.[11] His journals are sufficient monument to the persistence of this instinct. Day by day he wrote there—summaries of his reading, citations from it, comments on it; wood-thoughts; records

[6] *Life of Ralph Waldo Emerson*, 196–7.

[7] *Ralph Waldo Emerson*, 403–6.

[8] *My Study Windows: Emerson the Lecturer; A Fable for Critics.*

[9] *American Prose Writers: Emerson.*

[10] *Jour. IX*, 413.

[11] *Jour. I*, viii.

of conversations; anecdotes; stray metaphors; notes, sentences, and paragraphs for essays and lectures. When no thoughts came, he grieved and sought the cause. When inspiration did visit him, he watched its coming, its results, and its departure. Always, he thought about stylistic questions; his own and others' aims in expression; his own and their success and failure. And these thoughts he painstakingly recorded.

It has been my endeavor to classify and piece together these *disjecta membra*, hoping to show in them the homogeneity which I believe really resides there, and thus to evolve an Emersonian treatise on style. The materials are excellent. There has lived no other writer of power who has had so many definite, interesting, and valuable things to say about literary expression. Best of all, Emerson's attitude is not that of the textbook rhetorician; he deals not with formulas but with the living process of writing, in which he himself is every day engaged. It is important, but only secondarily so, that what he has to say gives the critic of his style an answer to what should be the critic's first question: What is the author himself trying to do? The real value in the assembling of this material is that it makes up a treatise of general interest to all who care about the art of writing. For though Emerson gained his ideas from first-hand experience and subordinated them to his philosophical tenets, many of them accord with the ideals which have governed writing from Aristotle's day to this.

Most of his comments on style connect themselves, as I have just said, with his philosophy, and gathering them and seeing them in their proper relations is, indeed, impossible without considering their underlying philosophical basis. His theories of literary expression cannot be divorced from the dualism which is inherent in transcendentalism, and from its corollary doctrines of the Symbol, and Each and All.

Definers of transcendentalism, especially of its New England manifestation, have been too prone to neglect what the chief of the American transcendentalists, Emerson, considered its central belief. Departing from Locke and agreeing with Kant, asserting that there are intuitive truths as well as those perceived by the senses, the transcendentalist of New England is a man of two worlds. He has an abiding faith that there is a sphere of sense and a sphere of spiritual perception; that two views of things are possible, the material and the ideal, and the ideal is paramount. For him some things seem, others are; some are apparent, others real; some finite, others infinite; some relative, others absolute. He is aware of the facts of consciousness, but he knows of truths above consciousness. And far more than the wordly facts he esteems the spiritual truths.

Indispensable aids by which the transcendentalist distinguishes the actual from the ideal are the Understanding and the Reason. These are lower and higher intellectual compartments that deal respectively with the concrete and with the loftily abstract; with the facts of experience and with intuitive truths. This world-old and nowadays pooh-poohed distinction, like the more inclusive one just repeated, which separates materialism from idealism, may be most conveniently and perhaps most accurately labeled Platonic. Concerning its modern application and sources it is advisable to quote from Emerson's significant letter to his brother Edward: "Do you draw the distinction of Milton, Coleridge, and the Germans between Reason and Understanding? . . . Reason is the highest faculty of the soul, what we mean often by the soul itself: it never *reasons*, never proves; it simply perceives, it is vision. The Understanding toils all the time, compares, contrives, adds, argues; near-sighted but strong-sighted, dwelling in the present, the expedient, the customary."[12] The transcendentalist, Emerson makes evident, has the advantage or disadvantage mentally of possessing both a green-shuttered habitation and an aery home.

Yet it is not enough to say this and to omit the relation which one has to the other. For the same fact may be looked at with the eye of Understanding, or with the eye of Reason—may be considered materially or ideally. "Every fact," Emerson says, "is related on one side to sensation, and on the other to morals. The game of thought is, on the appearance of one of these two sides, to find the other: given the upper, to find the under side. Nothing so thin but has these two faces, and when the observer has seen the obverse, he turns it over to see the reverse. Life is a pitching of this penny,—heads or tails."[13] And if the idealist always calls heads, he is not blind to the tail when it turns uppermost.

In fact, he derives from its appearance some notion of how the other side looks. After all, the many mansions are intelligible only because of the existence of earthly cottages. The transcendentalist subordinates, but he does not reject facts, experience, things that seem; he uses them symbolically. Reflected in the idealist's looking glass, temporalities serve as hints of things eternal, which would otherwise be incomprehensible. In other words, the transcendentalist, though he estimates the value of the apparent as low, does not therefore neglect it. Of supreme importance from the point of view of transcendental literary composition, he uses the apparent as language.

His attitude is this: he "admits the impressions of sense, admits their coherency, their use and beauty, and then asks the materialist for his grounds of assurance that things are as his senses represent them. But I, he says, affirm facts not affected by the illusions of sense, facts which are of the same nature as the faculty which reports them, and not liable to doubt; facts which in their first appearance to us assume a native

[12] *Memoir I*, 218.

[13] *Representative Men: Montaigne*, 150.

superiority to material facts, degrading these into a language by which the first are to be spoken."[14] The inferiority of the material facts is plain; so also is their figurative value as expression.

Of value in connection with expression, also, is the doctrine of the One and the Many, of Each and All. According to this, there exists above and runs through all things, natural and spiritual, a pervading essence, divine in nature. This is called by various names: the Eternal Unity, the One, the All, the Over-Soul. The One, being in all things, stands in peculiar relation to the many objects of nature and experience. Thorough understanding of its laws gives thorough understanding of the proper place and connection of all material phenomena. These laws therefore serve as a supreme means of classification. At the same time, the process may be reversed and the laws may in turn be arrived at by a proper attitude towards any material object. From every fact, from every object in Nature, it is possible to make generalizations regarding the class of facts or objects represented by the particular fact or object, or regarding other natural facts, or even regarding spiritual laws. In a drop of water, for instance, are concealed oceanic, physiological, universal, and eternal truths. From the Many the One is deduced; in variety identity is apparent; the All is in Each.

The knot which binds the theory of the One and the Many to the transcendental writer's use of worldly facts as spiritual symbols is not a complicated one. The worldly facts are the Many. Not only, then, may they be the language of any particular ideal thought, but in each symbol there is a universal as well as particular meaning, since every material fact points toward the divine unity. Perfection of style, therefore, is attained by the writer who knows and employs the relation between the earthly and the spiritual, and thus always suggests the Being immanent in them both. "Art," Emerson says, "expresses the one or the same by the different. Thought seeks to know unity in unity; poetry to show it by variety; that is, always by an object or symbol."[15] At the end of the *Journals* are written these lines from *Poesis Humana*, by Emerson's disciple, William Allingham:

> It shows in little much;
> And by an artful touch
> Conveys the hint of all.

Understanding and Reason; fact as fact and fact as symbol; the Many and the One, with their relationship to the idealist's attitude and his expression—all these corollaries have a basic dependence on the fundamental duality of transcendentalism. The subsequent chapters will show how this duality and its attendant principles control Emerson's

[14] *Nature, etc.: The Transcendentalist*, 330.
[15] *Representative Men: Plato*, 56.

notions about style, how they determine his theory and practice both with regard to diction and with regard to structural method.

The symbol is the idealist's chief means of communication; he thus rides on material things as the horses of his thought. Hence the symbol has its share in all the things that the transcendentalist considers good in expression; it is the inevitable constituent of poetry; the highest product of Reason and the Imagination. The correspondence between the natural and the spiritual which gives it this value makes it both man's language and God's. So it is that the man who lives close to Nature lives close to God and to divine inspiration and expression, and clothes his thoughts in figures which, by their trailing clouds of glory, attest their spiritual origin.

Though the symbol is preëminent in Emerson's theory of expression, its use cannot be completely comprehended without consideration also of its relation to the material things whose names it bears. Frequently, Emerson views expression as fitted to represent now the actual and now the ideal, and cleaves sharply between the two. But more often his purpose is to unite the actual and the ideal, to drive tandem the earthly and the heavenly, or, if you like, to hitch his wagon to a star. Such style he believes satisfactory to both sense and spirit; universal in its scope because it includes both poles of thought, the Reason and the Understanding.

These are general requirements. More specific is his insistence on adequacy, his demand for the right word and symbol in the right place. This is a requirement not easy to comply with, as he himself acknowledges, since it involves the attempt to keep in constant adjustment the relation between Nature and Spirit, the two sources from which his expression is drawn.

The same duality has another significant effect in connection with the theory of Each and All, and here is the explanation of Emerson's choice of vocabulary. From the fact that his language is homely as well as rich, his audience, which on the side of structure has few helps, is here conspicuously assisted. Since every object in Nature and every experience is inclusive and typical of eternity, any kind of material thing, and, in fact, the more common the better, is useful as substance for the transcendental writer. For him the simple, the everyday, in nature and in life, is capable of taking on divinity. And accordingly, that which is most frequently used for expressing the material fact—the idiomatic racy language of universal human experience, exact in its economy and caution—serves nobly also as the prophet's chariot of fire.

Thus dualism dominates Emerson's theories and practice with regard to diction. Not less profound and far-reaching is its influence, especially that of the theory of Each and All, on his structural method.

Artistic unity of structure is with Emerson a thing desired, but, unfortunately, a thing impossible of attainment. For Unity is with him spiritual as well as artistic; and unless his utterances relate themselves plainly to a scheme which is not a temporary makeshift but the scheme of the universe, he prefers to parallel them rather than force them into order and connection. He will not deal with the high inspirations of the Reason according to the methods of the Understanding. So long as he is serving the high cause of spiritual truth, he quite regardlessly sacrifices the infirm reader's craving for form and transitions.

He is forced to this not only by his thorough conviction that his utmost is to retail the eternal gossip for an hour, but also by his ambition to compile a natural history of the intellect. This ambition is the result of a zeal to imitate Bacon, modified in the direction of individualism by the example of Montaigne and the encouragement to self-reliance given by transcendentalism. As a result, he keeps journals, in which he records daily his momentary inspirations, and from these scattered utterances he composes his essays, his poems, his lectures—all his works. Here, he believes, is the only road open to him by which he can deliver in its purity the high spiritual thought which has come to him.

Thoroughly adequate combination and proportion of these fragments is, of course, impossible, though Emerson's success in assembling them is remarkable considering the circumstances. Some comfort in this situation comes to him from the Each and All theory, the very doctrine which has served to prevent him from classifying mechanically and practically, and has caused him to adopt the diary method in the first place. For it assures him that a lofty system, spiritual rather than material in character, is brought about from the mere accumulation of these data, since each part in turn epitomizes eternity, and since they are, after all, united spiritually as the result of their divinity of inspiration and their expression by one individual. Fortunately for the audience whose grasp is not consummately heavenly or philosophic, Emerson did not always thus console himself; but he did so often enough to make some of his essays distressingly aphoristic, and some of his poems pleasing because of their series of natural symbols, or tantalizing because of their occasional perfect lines.

Finally, sources and causes need to be considered. How did Emerson come to hold these theories of literary expression? From many quarters—Swedenborg, Wordsworth, Coleridge, Bacon, and Plato in especial—he gained encouragement for his innate dualism, and confidence in the sacred character of the symbol. With this he merged his increasing fondness for the simple and homely in style, his desire to make the usual word and thing do unusual stylistic work, and his wish to bend and shape the earthly to spiritual purposes. And here the influence of Montaigne and of sixteenth and seventeenth century English Platonists, as well as the independence bred by transcendentalism, has a part to play in affecting native tastes.

Though I shall try to show that dualism thus gives unified meaning to Emerson's comments on style, there is, I recognize, something false and unfair in the impression made by grouping according to any sort of plan that which was written without plan. In spite of the fact that philosophical theory recurs constantly as the basis for Emerson's discussions of style, he did not, if the truth be told, reduce and constrain them to these theories. The real value of this compilation must be, as I have said before, that it gathers in convenient form some of the concrete, pertinent, and entertaining things that Emerson has to say about the living process of writing. The reader, then, should feel at all times perfectly free to throw off the straitjacket of theory and transition and read as one who is interested in writing for writing's sake.

THE SYMBOL

The transcendentalist worships the symbol. He believes that the writer's principal power is the effective use of figures of speech. So deep and far-reaching, indeed, is his devotion that there is hardly anything of good repute connected with or a part of writing that is not intimately associated with the symbol. Reason, the noble mental faculty, embodies its reflections emblematically. Imagination is the power to symbolize. The man of genius is such because of his control of the symbol. Poetry presupposes the trope.

Before examining separately the reasons why the symbol is bone of bone and flesh of flesh with the reason, imagination, genius, and poetry, it is well to consider first the general ground on which the devotion is based. It is this: The material is the unique means by which the ideal may be expressed. Only the shadows of the ideal are available for the purposes of communicating it; only nature and human experience are provided as instruments by which the divine may be interpreted. "Man stands," according to Emerson, "on the point betwixt spirit and matter, and the native of both elements; the true thinker sees that one represents the other, that the world is the mirror of the soul, and that it is his office to show this beautiful relation. And this is literature."[1]

Since the world as a whole is thus emblematic, its parts and human experience must have a similar relationship to the individual ideas which make up spiritual thought. And indeed, figures of speech are, by virtue of this relationship, themselves "a low idealism. Idealism regards the world as symbolic, and all these symbols or forms as fugitive and convertible expressions. The power of the poet is in controlling these symbols; in using every fact in Nature, however great and stable, as a fluent symbol, and in measuring his strength by the facility with which he makes the mood of mind give its color to things."[2]

The fact converted to symbolic purposes being the ideal expression, it is obvious that the name of an object used typically is a higher form of utterance than the same name used positively. For the former expresses the ideal, and the latter the material or actual. "The primary use of a fact is low; the secondary use, as it is a figure or illustration of my thought, is the real worth. First the fact; second its impression, or what I think of it."[3] Words used in their ordinary sense may represent accurately worldly

[1] *Memoir* II, 716.

[2] *Natural History of Intellect: Art and Criticism*, 300.

[3] *Letters, etc.: Poetry and Imagination, Poetry*, 11.

truth. Figures of speech do more: they help the writer to represent accurately spiritual truth.

It is now easy to see why the symbol has a share in everything the transcendentalist holds dear: the reason, the imagination, genius, and poetry. It is plain that the reason, the ideal part of the mind, must be capable of seeing things emblematically. It is not surprising, either, that to the executive power of phrasing them emblematically there should be applied the term imagination. This Emerson defines as: "the nomination of the causal facts, the laws of the soul, by the physical facts. All physical facts are words for spiritual facts, and Imagination, by naming them, is the Interpreter, showing us the unity of the world."[4] And, to proceed one step farther, he in whom this capacity for ideal vision and utterance is constantly and powerfully present, has genius. "The term 'genius,' when used with emphasis," says Emerson, "implies imagination; use of symbols, figurative speech. A deep insight will always, like Nature, ultimate its thought in a thing."[5]

The same basic conceptions apply to the relationship between the symbol and poetry. Poetry, in Emerson's philosophy, is differentiated from prose by the fact that whereas prose may be the expression of the actual, poetry must be the expression of the ideal. And being ideal expression, it is, of course, symbolic. How poetry is distinguished from prose and consanguineous with the Reason, the symbol, and idealism in general is sufficiently indicated in these sentences from the Journals: "Poetry preceded prose, as the form of sustained thought, as Reason, whose vehicle poetry is, precedes the Understanding. When you assume the rhythm of verse and the analogy of nature, it is making proclamation, 'I am now freed from the trammels of the Apparent; I speak from the Mind.' "[6]

Thus the sacred character of the symbol, the material expression of divine truth, causes it to pervade literature. Examination may now be made of the grounds for Emerson's belief that the inevitable expression of the metaphysical is the physical, and of the consequences of this belief. That the spiritual seeks symbolic utterance there are both human and divine indications. Not only does Nature serve man as a means of embodying abstract truth; it is also God's language. Philology gives testimony to the one; science to the other. Psychology next lends its aid in making clear the connection between Man, Spirit, and the Symbol; for it shows the desirability of a simple life in natural surroundings as a means of bringing up in the writer's mind apt and meaningful symbols. And since achievement of adequate expression depends upon such conditions, Emerson sees value in the symbol as a certifier of truth and an establisher

[4] *Jour.* IX, 127.
[5] *Letters, etc.: Poetry and Imagination, Poetry*, 17.
[6] *Jour.* III, 492.

of conviction. Most powerful, he believes, is the inspirational effect which the symbol has by virtue of the fact that it is itself inspired.

For the belief that man goes to Nature when he wishes to express the abstract or the holy, Emerson finds philological warrant. He points it out in *Nature* at the beginning of the chapter entitled *Language*. "Words," he says, "are signs of natural facts." He here states what is familar even to novices in philology, that almost every word was at one time a figure of speech, and especially that "every word which is used to express a moral or intellectual fact, if traced to its root, is found to be borrowed from some material appearance." The very word *Spirit* "primarily means *wind*." Thus language is inherently symbolic, "fossil poetry,"[7] as Emerson calls it.

But Emerson does not stop here. He goes farther than most philologists, however enthusiastic. He does not content himself with the statement that the human mind finds in Nature a correspondence with its own thoughts, and utilizes this for purposes of expression. If this were the only aspect of the transcendental attitude toward Nature and its effect on style, the matter would be clear enough. It is complicated, however, by the fact that the transcendentalist regards Nature not only as man's language, but as God's. "There seems to be a necessity in spirit to manifest itself in material forms; and day and night, river and storm, beast and bird, acid and alkali, preëxist in necessary Ideas in the mind of God, and are what they are by virtue of preceding affections in the world of spirit. A Fact is the end or last issue of spirit. The visible creation is the terminus or the circumference of the invisible world."[8]

That Nature is a mode of divine speech is exemplified, Emerson believes, in the correspondence between ethical and scientific laws. "The laws of moral nature answer to those of matter as face to face in a glass. . . .The axioms of physics translate the laws of ethics. Thus, 'the whole is greater than its part'; 'reaction is equal to action' "; [—axioms which have in addition to their physical sense possibilities as expression, respectively, of Emerson's belief in the relation of the One to the Many, and the doctrine of Compensation.]

"In like manner, the memorable words of history and the proverbs of nations consist usually of a natural fact, selected as a picture or parable of a moral truth. . . . 'Tis hard to carry a full cup even; . . . . Long-lived trees make roots first . . . .In their primary sense these are trivial facts, but we repeat them for the value of their analogical import."[9]

Thus it is that science fails, in Emerson's opinion, if it merely peeps and botanizes, merely accumulates data. Its aim should be the discovery

[7] *Essays II: The Poet*, 22.
[8] *Nature, etc.: Language*, 34–5.
[9] *Nature, etc.: Language*, 33.

of general physical laws, for through knowledge of these we gain insight into spiritual problems also. Investigation of the Many is only justified for its bearing on the One. In idealism, Emerson thinks, resides the connection between literature and language on one side, and science on the other. Emerson himself points out that Goethe's universal insight made it possible for him to make contributions to science.[10] Conversely, it is worthy of remark that Tyndall, the great scientist, known for "his strong, picturesque mode of seizing and expressing things,"[11] acknowledged his indebtedness to Emerson; and that W. D. Whitney, who more than any other philologist has emphasized that the origin of language was symbolic, was himself a scientist of no little reputation.

If, therefore, it can be demonstrated that nature is simultaneously human and divine language, human expression is adequate only when the individual mind harmonizes with the Over-Soul; when the Reason, rather than the Understanding, is operative. For this belief there is psychological basis. In the happy hours of communion with the unseen, there appears before the mind a symbol, and usually a proper symbol, for every thought. All past experience is a fund, which, in these felicitous intervals, can be drawn upon.[12]

Emerson's first writing of this thought in his *Journals* is followed by some interesting examples drawn from his own experience. He had been setting down the account of a conversation in which he had said that a man's "Wilfulness may determine the character of moments, but his Will determines that of years. . . .

"While I thus talked, I *saw* some crude *symbols* of the thought with the mind's eye,—as it were, a mass of grass or weeds in a stream, of which the spears or blades shot out from the mass in every direction, but were immediately curved round to float all in one direction. When presently the conversation changed to the subject of Thomas à Kempis's popularity, and how Aristotle and Plato come safely down, as if God brought them in his hand (though at no time are there more than five or six men who read them), and of the Natural Academy by which the exact value of every book is determined, maugre all hindrance or furtherance; then saw I, as I spoke, the old pail in the Summer Street kitchen with potatoes swimming in it, some at the top, some in the midst, and some lying at the bottom; and I spoiled my fine thought by saying that books take their place according to their specific gravity 'as surely as potatoes in a tub.' "[13]

Exaltation of thought finds vent not only in suitable symbols, but also in fitting illustration. "The way in which Burke or Sheridan or Webster

[10] *Representative Men: Goethe*, 274–5.

[11] *Encyclopaedia Britannica*, XXVII, 499.

[12] *Nature, etc.: Language*, 30–31.

[13] *Jour.* III, 527-8.

surprises us," Emerson says in his essay on *Memory*, ". . . is by his always having a sharp tool that fits the present use. . . . The more he is heated, the wider he sees; he seems to remember all he ever knew."[14] Emerson's style is similarly vivified. Like many profound thinkers and writers—Montaigne and Burton notably—he is wealthy in illustration; he heaps up instances of his point. "Rammed with life," the phrase which he borrows from Ben Jonson to describe Plutarch's "rapid and crowded style,"[15] could well be applied to his own writing.

To the state of mind which makes apposite symbol and illustration possible, two elements contribute; a life in natural surroundings, and the desire to express truth which follows upon simplicity of life and character.

By getting close to Nature, we approach divinity, since Nature is an externization of spirit. And, because our expression depends on our experience, the country is most likely to cause those mental impressions which in later years will have their effect in the purest of language, symbols, that is, which depend directly on Nature. Emerson emphasizes "the advantage which the country life possesses, for a powerful mind, over the artificial and curtailed life of cities," and declares that the natural images, insensibly received into the mind, will, "at the call of a noble sentiment," "reappear in their morning lustre, as fit symbols and words of the thoughts which the passing events shall awaken."[16]

Emerson himself spent most of the early part of his life in Boston, and came to the ruralities of Concord in his early thirties—a most impressionable and often decisive age so far as style is concerned. In discussing the sources of his devotion to the symbol, I shall try to show how this change of surroundings co-operates with other influences. Here it is sufficient to point out its direct effect on his own style. He came to Nature late, as one who, never having been in love, falls into it suddenly at the age of thirty-five. In a letter at this time, he wrote: "A sunset, a forest, a snow-storm, a certain river-view, are more to me than many friends, and do ordinarily divide my day with my books."[17] Stiltedness and formality—result of his ministerial office and his youthful admiration for the flowers of eloquence—gave way to a poetic warmth great enough to justify the name of "rhapsody" often applied to his first book, *Nature*. And in regard to his next book he writes in his Journals: "All my thoughts are foresters. I have

[14] *Natural History of Intellect*, 98.

[15] *Lectures, etc.: Plutarch*, 300–301.

[16] *Nature, etc.: Language*, 31. Daniel Webster in a letter dated September 29, 1845 wrote thus of New Hampshire: "I am attracted to this particular spot by very strong feelings. It is the scene of my early years; and it is thought [by Emerson?], and I believe truly, that these scenes come back upon us with renewed interest and more strength of feeling as we find years running over us." F. B. Sanborn: Henry D. Thoreau.

[17] *Memoir* I, 236-7.

scarce a day-dream on which the breath of the pines has not blown, and their shadows waved. Shall I not then call my little book Forest Essays?"[18]

"The poet," Emerson writes, "should walk in the fields, drawn on by new scenes, supplied with vivid pictures and thoughts, until insensibly the recollection of his home was crowded out of his mind, and all memory obliterated, and he was led in triumph by Nature.

"When he spoke of the stars he should be innocent of what he said; for it seemed that the stars, as they rolled over him, mirrored themselves in his mind as in a deep well, and it was their image and not his thought that you saw."[19]

This intimate kinship between style and Nature engendered by country life is impossible for the man whose character has been warped from native simplicity. The writer removed from direct contact with Nature by artificial and complex social conditions must express himself falsely and weakly, for the truest language, the figurative, is for him borrowed finery, superposed ornamentation, rather than symbols that tell the truth by being an integral part of the fact which they describe. "Hundreds of writers," Emerson declares, "may be found in every long-civilized nation who for a short time believe and make others believe that they see and utter truths, who do not of themselves clothe one thought in its natural garment, but who feed unconsciously on the language created by the primary writers of the country, those, namely, who hold primarily on nature."[20]

Herein, for instance, lies the weakness of the literature of the neoclassical eighteenth century. "Pope and Johnson and Addison," Emerson asserts, "write as if they had never seen the face of the country, but had only read of trees and rivers in books."[21] And again: "Pope and his school wrote poetry fit to put round frosted cake."[22] In this respect at least he believes Webster is superior to Burke, for "Burke's imagery is, much of it, got from books, and so is a secondary formation. Webster's is all primary."[23] And the remedy, once more, is this: "Let a man make the woods and fields his books; then at the hour of passion his thoughts will invest themselves spontaneously with natural imagery."[24]

The worth of immediate reference to Nature is taken advantage of, also, by the orator whose speech gains in pertinency and in truth through connection with out-of-door realities. "Webster," Emerson notes, "never loses sight of his relation to Nature. The Day is always a part of him.

[18] *Jour.* V, 513-4.
[19] *Jour.* VI, 453.
[20] *Nature, etc.: Language,* 30.
[21] *Jour.* IV, 259.
[22] *English Traits: Literature,* 255.
[23] *Jour.* III, 567.
[24] Ibid.

'But, Mr. President, the shades of evening which close around us, admonish us to conclude,' he said at Cambridge."[25]

The psychological connection between Truth, Nature, and expression is shown in the fact, Emerson believes, "that the advocate of the good cause finds a wealth of arguments and illustrations on his way. He stands for Truth, and Truth and Nature help him unexpectedly and irresistibly at every step. All the felicities of example, of imagery, of admirable poetry, old religion, new thought, the analogies of science, throng to him and strengthen his position. Nay, when we had to praise John Brown of Osawatomie, I remember . . . what a multitude of fine verses of old poetry fitted him exactly, and appeared to have been prophetically written for the occasion."[26]

Nature, then, is the source through which the writer derives the ability to express himself figuratively in nearest accordance with the divine language. For philology, philosophy, natural science, and psychology unite to furnish indications that Nature serves both God and man as means of communication. It is clear, too, that the highest type of ideal expression, adequate symbols, is available to the writer who recognizes Nature as divine utterance, and comes close to its message by a life as near as possible to it, and of conforming simplicity.

If Nature is the source, and the source itself has intimate kinship with the divine, it is therefore conversely true that the writer's symbols furnish a test by which both he and his audience may determine the validity of his utterances, and the quality of mind from which they issue.

"A happy symbol is a sort of evidence that your thought is just. I had rather have a good symbol of my thought, or a good analogy, than the suffrage of Kant or Plato. If you agree with me, or if Locke or Montesquieu agree, I may yet be wrong; but if the elm-tree thinks the same thing, if running water, if burning coal, if crystals, if alkalies, in their several fashions say what I say, it must be true."[27]

In the symbol Emerson found a means of judging depth of mentality. "An index or mercury of intellectual proficiency," he says, "is the perception of identity."[28] "In meeting a new student." he writes in his Journals, "I incline to ask him, Do you know any deep man? Has any one furnished you with a new image? For to see the world representatively, implies high gifts."[29] One symbol, indeed, may be the clue to genius. "'Tis a good mark of any genius, a single novel expression of the identity. Thus Lord Brooke's

'So words should sparkes be of those fires they strike.'

[25] *Jour.* IV, 172.
[26] *Jour.* X, 107-8.
[27] *Letters, etc.: Poetry and Imagination, Poetry*, 13.
[28] *Essays* I: *Intellect*, 340.
[29] *Jour.* VIII, 517.

Or Donne's

'That one would almost say her body thought.' "[30]

Since figures of speech immediately dependent on Nature convince the hearer or reader of their high origin and thus of their truth, the symbol is of great value persuasively. Even on a low plane, the directness of its relationship to Nature accounts for a definiteness, a concreteness of feeling on the part of the audience; they are sure of the author's fidelity to the fact. And when the symbol is of higher origin, is truly spiritual, the loftiness of the region from which it wings its flight assures the audience of the reality of the inspiration, and at the same time their spirits also are lifted to the exhilarating ether. With such elevation comes absolute confidence.

"The orator must be, to a certain extent, a poet. We are such imaginative creatures that nothing so works on the human mind, barbarous or civil, as a trope. Condense some daily experience into a glowing symbol, and an audience is electrified. They feel as if they already possessed some right and power over a fact which they can detach and so completely master in thought. It is a wonderful aid to the memory which carries away the image and never loses it. A popular assembly, like the House of Commons, or the French Chamber, or the American Congress, is commanded by these two powers,—first by a fact, then by skill of statement. Put the argument into a concrete shape, into an image,—some hard phrase, round and solid as a ball, which they can see and handle and carry home with them,—and the cause is half won."[31]

With the same effect as symbols are illustrations, specific instances. Again the fusion of the material with the mental produces conviction. "I cannot hear a sermon," declares Emerson, "without being struck by the fact that amid drowsy series of sentences what a sensation a historical fact, a biographical name, a sharply objective illustration makes! Why will not the preacher heed the admonitions of the momentary silence of his congregation and (often what is shown him) that this particular sentence is all they carry away? Is he not taught hereby that the synthesis is to all grateful, and to most indispensable, of abstract thought and concrete body? Principles should be verified by the adducing of facts and sentiments incorporated by their appropriate imagery."[32]

More far-reaching is the effect of the symbol which embodies high spiritual truths. It is durable and pervasive. It dominates literature and makes it popular. It determines national destinies. And because of its ideal nature it breaks the boundaries of sense and opens the everlasting gates of spirit.

[30] *Jour.* VIII, 46.
[31] *Society and Solitude: Eloquence*, 90.
[32] *Jour.* IV, 169-170.

"A good symbol is the best argument, and is a missionary to persuade thousands." "A figurative statement arrests attention, and is remembered and repeated. How often has a phrase of this kind made a reputation. Pythagoras's Golden Sayings were such, and Socrates's, and Mirabeau's, and Burke's, and Bonaparte's. . . . There is no more welcome gift to men than a new symbol. That satiates, transports, converts them. They assimilate themselves to it, deal with it in all ways, and it will last a hundred years. Then comes a new genius, and brings another."[33]

To this pure pleasure which the symbol affords, all men are subject. "All men are so far poets. When people tell me they do not relish poetry, and bring me Shelley, or Aikin's Poets, or I know not what volumes of rhymed English, to show that it has no charm, I am quite of their mind. But this dislike of the books only proves their liking of poetry. For they relish Æsop,—cannot forget him or not use him; bring them Homer's Iliad, and they like that; or the Cid, and that rings well; read to them from Chaucer, and they reckon him an honest fellow. Lear and Macbeth and Richard III. they know pretty well without guide. Give them Robin Hood's ballads or Griselda, or Sir Andrew Barton, or Sir Patrick Spens, or Chevy Chase, or Tam O'Shanter, and they like these well enough. . . . They like poetry without knowing it as such. They like to go to the theatre and be made to weep; to Faneuil Hall, and be taught by Otis, Webster, or Kossuth, or Phillips, what great hearts they have, what tears, what new possible enlargements to their narrow horizons."[34]

Thus the democratic literature is the symbolic. And there are other symbols, more peculiarly of the people, by the people, and for the people, which are emblematic of party belief, and even of patriotism. "In our political parties," says Emerson, "compute the power of badges and emblems. See the great ball which they roll from Baltimore to Bunker hill! In the political processions, Lowell goes in a loom, and Lynn in a shoe, and Salem in a ship. Witness the cider-barrel, the log-cabin, the hickory-stick, the palmetto, and all the cognizances of party. See the power of national emblems. Some stars, lilies, leopards, a crescent, a lion, an eagle, or other figure which came into credit God knows how, on an old rag of bunting, blowing in the wind on a fort at the ends of the earth, shall make the blood tingle under the rudest or the most conventional exterior. The people fancy they hate poetry, and they are all poets and mystics!"[35]

Accompanying and reinforcing the persuasive influence of the symbol is its lifting power. By providing a means of escape from the world of shows to the world of realities it awakens joy and gratitude. "Mark the

[33] *Letters, etc.: Poetry and Imagination, Poetry,* 12–3.
[34] *Letters, etc.: Poetry and Imagination, Imagination,* 25–6.
[35] *Essays* II: *The Poet,* 16–7.

delight of an audience in an image. When some familiar truth or fact appears in a new dress, mounted as on a fine horse, equipped with a grand pair of ballooning wings, we cannot enough testify our surprise and pleasure."[36] "The metamorphosis excites in the beholder an emotion of joy. The use of symbols has a certain power of emancipation and exhilaration for all men. . . . We are like persons who come out of a cave or cellar into the open air. . . . Poets are thus liberating gods. Men have really got a new sense, and found within their world another world, or nest of worlds; for, the metamorphosis once seen, we divine that it does not stop."[37]

For this translation to the heights which the symbolizer makes possible, his reward is the greatest: his work is permanent. "This emancipation is dear to all men, and the power to impart it, as it must come from greater depth and scope of thought, is a measure of intellect. Therefore all books of the imagination endure, all which ascend to that truth that the writer sees nature beneath him, and uses it as his exponent. Every verse or sentence possessing this virtue will take care of its own immortality."[38]

For Emerson, the dependence of literature on the symbol is complete. Nature, the inevitable material means of expressing the ideal, is not only man's language, but God's. By a life close to Nature, and in harmony with it, the writer stores his mind with images, which, at the hour appointed, fitly clothe his thought. The symbol thus derived is held, by virtue of its divine source, in the highest regard; the writer's symbolically expressed ideas are received with the glad trust and exaltation of mood which welcome the literature of genius. The light of God's countenance has shone on the face of the material, and has transfigured it.

[36] *Letters, etc.: Poetry and Imagination, Poetry*, 12–3.
[37] *Essays* II: *The Poet*, 30.
[38] *Essays* II: *The Poet*, 33–4.

THE FACT AND THE SYMBOL

The symbol, the noble because the ideal form of expression, Emerson has much to say about independently. In the preceding section it has been clear enough that he often considers it apart from the material fact whose name it employs, and does not take into account that this same name is used, on the material plane, without ulterior meaning. Yet to disregard, even to fail to lay considerable stress on the relationship between the fact and the symbol, would be to neglect the very fundamentals of Emerson's theory of style. For the complex but intimate connection between them has two important effects. First, it is woven through and through Emerson's demand that expression should be the exact and final representation of the thing it is trying to describe. Second, in combination with the doctrine of the One and the Many, the relationship between fact and symbol makes possible for Emerson the belief that language may be simple, idiomatic and reticent, at the same time that it is symbolic and even intense. Discussion of these two effects comes properly under the headings of *Adequacy* and *Each and All.*

1. Adequacy

The transcendentalist does not spurn the impressions of sense. He regards the emanations of the Reason as sublime in their effect and origin; but however heavenly are the regions he is capable of inhabiting, he is from time to time conscious of his feet firmly planted on the earth. Hence his style and his theories about style are a compound. At times he grips the fact; at others he cherishes the symbol; most frequently he takes middle ground, and in the midst of his worship of the symbol does not forget the fact behind it.

There are occasions when he follows what Emerson calls "the rule of positive and superlative." "As long as you deal with sensible objects in the sphere of sense, call things by their right names. But every man may be, and some men are, raised to a platform whence he sees beyond sense to moral and spiritual truth; when he no longer sees snow as snow, or horses as horses, but only sees or names them representatively for those interior facts which they signify. This is the way the poets use them. And in that exalted state, the mind deals very easily with great and small material things, and strings worlds like beads upon its thought."[1]

Common sense regards a spade as a spade; idealism may consider it emblematic, let us say, of Carlyle's philosophy of work. Actually, pigs is pigs; transcendentally, they may represent materialism.

[1] *Jour.* VIII, 520.

But usually the expression of the ideal is not so sharply differentiated from the expression of the material. The transcendental writer remembers that he does not always breathe thin air. Though he has a share of the divine spirit, he is also human; the elements are mixed in him. The same is true of his readers. His style, then, must be correspondingly blended of the everyday and the eternal. This being the case, he finds comfort and aid in the fact that he may often express himself materially and ideally at the same time; since the material, the only means by which the ideal may be expressed, therefore always suggests the ideal. His style may be "the imaginative-practical." Since "Imagination is suspected, the mechanical is despised," he may "write the solid *and* the ethereal, for the divine."[2] "The poet, like the electric rod, must reach from a point nearer the sky than all surrounding objects, down to the earth, and into the dark wet soil, or neither is of use. The poet must not only converse with pure thought, but he must demonstrate it almost to the senses. His words must be pictures, his verses must be spheres and cubes, to be seen and smelled and handled. His fable must be a good story, and its meaning must hold as pure truth. In the debates on the Copyright Bill, in the English Parliament, Mr. Sergeant Wakley, the coroner, quoted Wordsworth's poetry in derision, and asked the roaring House of Commons what that meant, and whether a man should have public reward for writing such stuff. Homer, Horace, Milton and Chaucer would defy the coroner. Whilst they have wisdom to the wise, he would see that to the external they have external meaning. Coleridge excellently said of poetry, that poetry must first be good sense; as a palace might well be magnificent, but first it must be a house."[3]

But this is not all. Not only should these two tests of fitness be satisfied, but working with them is a requirement of stylistic accuracy, in general and applied to the single word or phrase. Emerson is as rigid in his demand for the right word as Flaubert. He is extreme enough to say: "No man can write well who thinks there is any choice of words for him. The laws of composition are as strict as those of sculpture and architecture. There is always one line that ought to be drawn, or one proportion that should be kept, and every other line or proportion is wrong, and so far wrong as it deviates from this. So in writing, there is always a right word, and every other than that is wrong."[4]

Without stringent, painstaking revision, the right word is in many cases impossible of attainment. Emerson polished his writings religiously. Concerning revision he writes: "The address to the Divinity School is published, and they are printing the Dartmouth Oration. The correction

[2] *Jour.* VII, 31.

[3] *Natural History of Intellect: Papers from the Dial, Europe and European Books*, 366–7. Dr. Easley S. Jones has called my attention to the parallelism of this conception and Barrett Wendell's distinction between denotation and connotation.

[4] *Jour.* II, 401.

of these two pieces for the press has cost me no small labor. . . . But negligence in the author is inexcusable. I know and will know no such thing as haste in composition."[5] And in another passage: "If that worthy ancient king, in the school-books, who offered a reward to the author of a new pleasure could make his proclamation anew, I should put in for the first prize. I would tell him to write an oration, and then print it, and, setting himself diligently to the correction, let him strike out a blunder and insert the right word just ere the press falls, and he shall know a new pleasure."[6]

The right word is secured through an exact adjustment between words and the things they express. This requirement raises perplexing difficulties to beset the writer. In the first place, the problem of expression is always complicated by the fact that some things are actual, and some are spiritual; the writer must be accurate on either level, or even, as we have seen, on both simultaneously. In the second place, expression may be considered as representing either the processes of the writer's mind, or the facts and the experience which furnish the material for these processes. Writing may be a picture of the writer's mind; or it may be a picture of Nature. In either case, of course, duality has its influence in determining what is accurate. For the writer's mind is made up of Understanding and Reason; and facts and experience may be utilized for expressing either the impressions of sense, or spiritual truth, or once more, both. In the third place, as is perhaps sufficiently suggested by the foregoing, the limitations of language must be considered. Emerson speaks at times of making the word fit the thing, but at other times, more ambitiously, he speaks of making words one with things. Identity of word and object is only momentarily possible, however, for the object, as a part of Nature, expresses divine truth, and only in moments of communion with the Over-Soul, moments of ecstasy, is it possible for the human individual to speak divinely. Hence ordinarily words aim to describe, rather than *are* the thing. This aim is stringent enough in its demands, and the occasions are frequent and perhaps usual when words do not succeed even in describing, but are content merely to suggest.

a. Accuracy

Detailed consideration of these notions will serve to clarify, though it may not succeed in showing entire consistency. At the outset it should be plain that whatever the difficulties and whatever the complications, Emerson admires accurate expression wherever he finds it: he calls it "the most precious beauty."[7] He extols Shakspeare in this regard: "One

[5] *Jour.* V, 21.
[6] *Jour.* V, 12.
[7] *Jour.* X, 229.

would say Shakspeare must have been a thousand years old when he wrote his first piece; so thoroughly is his thought familiar to him, so solidly worded, as if it were already a proverb, and not only hereafter to become one. Shakspeare is nothing but a large utterance . . . a wonderful symbolizer and expressor, who has no rival in all ages."[8] Milton's versatile precision he praises almost as highly: "Milton's mind seems to have no thought or emotion which refused to be recorded. His mastery of his native tongue was more than to use it as well as any other; he cast it into new forms. He uttered in it things unheard before. Not imitating but rivalling Shakspeare, he scattered, in tones of prolonged and delicate melody, his pastoral and romantic fancies; then, soaring into unattempted strains, he made it capable of an unknown majesty, and bent it to express every trait of beauty, every shade of thought; and searched the kennel and jakes as well as the palaces of sound for the harsh discords of his polemic wrath."[9]

Emerson, it is true, sometimes feels the element of illusion in expression and acknowledges that it can never really take the place of the spiritual life which language at its best strives to represent. "I," he says, "who have all my life heard any number of orations and debates, read poems and miscellaneous books, conversed with many geniuses, am still the victim of any new page; and if Marmaduke, or Hugh, or Moosehead, or any other, invent a new style or mythology, I fancy that the world will be all brave and right if dressed in these colors, which I had not thought of. Then at once I will daub with this new paint; but it will not stick. 'Tis like the cement which the peddler sells at the door; he makes broken crockery hold with it, but you can never buy of him a bit of the cement which will make it hold when he is gone."[10] And with this unsatisfying aspect of literature in mind he may write ironically: "Naming, yes, that is the office of the newspapers of the world, these famous editors from Moses, Homer, Confucius, and so on, down to Goethe and Kant: they name what the people have already done, and the thankful people say, 'Doctor, 'tis a great comfort to know the disease whereof I die.' "[11] But the superiority of the fact used as symbolic language to the fact considered as the object of sensation is so great that he can also write: "I don't know but I value the name of a thing, that is, the true poet's name for it, more than the thing. If I can get the right word for the moon, or about it,—the word that suggests to me and to all men its humane and universal beauty and significance,—then I have what I want of it, and shall not desire that a road may be made from my garden to the moon, or that the gift of this elephant may be made over to me."[12]

[8] *Natural History of Intellect: Art and Criticism*, 294.
[9] *Natural History of Intellect: Milton*, 260–1.
[10] *Conduct of Life: Illusions*, 316–7.
[11] *Jour.* VI, 330.
[12] *Jour.* X, 175-6.

This cherishing of the ideal expression does not, in Emerson's case, preclude a fondness for satisfactory expression of the actual. Sometimes he craves relief from the fugitive impalpabilities of idealism. In any case he is man of this world and artist enough to delight in the solid footing which he finds in Montaigne; in several English authors; and in the American orators, Webster and Phillips. And indeed, the hard certainty and concreteness which is the effect of accurate recording of physical facts is a quality which Emerson believes the expression of the ideal, the symbol, may well strive for.

Emerson writes thus of the effect of too much reading in the Platonists: "We have too many fine books, and as those who have too much cake and candy long for a brown crust, so we like the *Albany Cultivator*."[13] And again he confesses mild revolt when he declares: "Men are weathercocks and like nothing long. We are disgusted with history because it is precise, external, and indigent. But take up Behmen, or Swedenborg, or Carlyle even, or any other who will write history mystically, and we wish straightway for French science and facts recorded agreeably to the common sense of mankind."[14]

Herein lies part of the reason for his sympathy with Montaigne. The essay devoted to him in *Representative Men* includes several paragraphs written in sympathetic comprehension of Montaigne's desire not to "overstate the dry fact"; to assure his reader that "whatever you get here shall smack of the earth and of real life, sweet, or smart, or stinging."

Emerson finds English literature deficient in idealism; but at the same time he is appreciative of its success in realistic expression. Swift "describes his fictitious persons as if for the police. Defoe has no insecurity or choice. Hudibras has the same hard mentality,—keeping the truth at once to the senses and to the intellect. . . . Chaucer's hard painting of his Canterbury pilgrims satisfies the senses."[15]

Exactness in expression of the fact is an indispensable part of eloquence. "Eloquence must be grounded on the plainest narrative. Afterwards, it may warm itself until it exhales symbols of every kind and color, speaks only through the most poetic forms; but, first and last, it must still be at bottom a biblical statement of fact."[16] Emerson praises Wendell Phillips because "the capital lesson" of eloquence may be learned from him that "the first and the second and the third part of the art is, to keep your feet always firm on a fact."[17] Webster is similarly commendable. Emerson

[13] *Jour.* VI, 244.

[14] *Jour.* VII, 20.

[15] *English Traits: Literature*, 234.

[16] *Society and Solitude: Eloquence*, 93.

[17] *Jour.* VI, 542.

speaks of his "daylight statement";[18] and tells us that in the Bunker Hill Address, he "hugged his fact . . . close."[19]

Superior as an expressor of the fact to any of the authors or speakers mentioned is, in Emerson's opinion, Carlyle—"a better painter in the Dutch style than we have had in literature before. It is terrible—his closeness and fidelity: he copies that which never was seen before. It is like seeing your figure in a glass. It is an improvement in writing as strange as Daguerre's in picture, and rightly fell in the same age with that."[20] Emerson uses many phrases to suggest the variety and at the same time the precision of Carlyle's style: "I see," he writes in regard to *Frederick the Great*, "the eyes of the writer looking into my eyes; all the way, chuckling with undertones and puns and winks and shrugs and long commanding glances, and stereoscoping every figure that passes, and every hill, river, wood, hummock, and pebble in the long perspective."[21] To the same effect he writes elsewhere that in Carlyle's book "You have no board interposed between you and the writer's mind, but he talks flexibly, now high, now low, in loud emphasis, in undertones, then laughs till the walls ring, then calmly moderates, then hints, or raises an eyebrow. He has gone nigher to the wind than any other craft."[22]

What of Emerson's own success as a Dutch painter? Though the greater part of his writing is idealistic, he does not meet with failure when it is his duty to describe the material. His historical addresses serve their purpose satisfactorily. *English Traits* shows keenness of sight, as well as of insight. He characterizes with precision the mingled earthliness and spirituality of his uncle, the Rev. Ezra Ripley, D.D.[23] He interprets racily and understandingly such middle-of-the-road seekers after truth as Socrates[24] and Montaigne.[25] The lineaments of the Devil, even, seem recognizable in his portrait of Mephistopheles.[26] And in the essay on *Fate* in *Conduct of Life* he clinches grimly with Grendel and comes away victorious.

Often Emerson uses such collections of fact-words as mark the just-quoted passages descriptive of Carlyle's style: "Undertones and puns and winks and shrugs." He may employ them either to create the effect of exactness in representing the actual; or, contrariwise, to show the illusoriness of the impressions of sense. He takes his stand on terra firma

[18] *Miscellanies: The Fugitive Slave Law—Address at Concord*, 202.

[19] *Miscellanies: The Fugitive Slave Law—Lecture at New York*, 222.

[20] *Jour.* VIII, 250-1.

[21] *Jour.* IX, 195-6.

[22] *Natural History of Intellect: Art and Criticism*, 299.

[23] *Lectures, etc.*

[24] *Representative Men: Plato*, 70–75.

[25] *Representative Men.*

[26] *Representative Men: Goethe*, 276–7.

and writes: "The stuff of all countries is just the same. Do you suppose there is any country where they do not scald milk-pans, and swaddle the infants, and burn the brushwood, and broil the fish?"[27] He takes firm hold, too, in this sentence: "England is aghast at the disclosure of her fraud in the adulteration of food, of drugs and of almost every fabric in her mills and shops; finding that milk will not nourish, nor sugar sweeten, nor bread satisfy, nor pepper bite the tongue, nor glue stick."[28] Sometimes, however, Emerson uses such concrete series to suggest that, after all, the facts are transitory and unsubstantial. As when he says that man's "operations taken together are so insignificant, a little chipping, baking, patching, and washing, that in an impression so grand as that of the world on the human mind, they do not vary the result."[29]

Emerson admires and practises the expression of actual facts. But the truer expression, the more exact, is the symbolic—the ideal. "Trueness of sight" is displayed, he says, "in using such words as show that the man was an eye-witness, and not a repeater of what was told. Thus, the girl who said 'the earth was agee'; Lord Bacon when he speaks of exploding gunpowder as 'a fiery wind blowing with that expansive force.' "[30]

The writer should not, however, be satisfied because through the symbol he attains a nobler adequacy of utterance. The impression of stability which is produced by fidelity to the fact on the material plane can be reproduced in the realm of the ideal with even greater surety of effect. "There are two powers of the imagination," according to Emerson. One is the power to symbolize; "and the other . . . is . . . the tenaciousness of an image, cleaving unto it and letting it not go, and, by the treatment, demonstrating that this figment of thought is as palpable and objective to the poet as is the ground on which he stands, or the walls of houses about him."[31] Or, in other words, "The problem of the poet is to unite freedom with precision; to give the pleasure of color, and be not less the most powerful of sculptors."[32]

Here resides the strength of Dante and of Shakspeare. "Dante was free imagination,—all wings,—yet he wrote like Euclid."[33] "Dante's imagination," Emerson says, "is the nearest to hands and feet that we have seen. He clasps the thought as if it were a tree or a stone, and describes as mathematically. I once found Page the painter modelling his figures in clay, Ruth and Naomi, before he painted them on canvas.

[27] *Conduct of Life: Culture*, 145–6.
[28] *English Traits: Wealth*, 167–8.
[29] *Nature, etc.: Introduction*, 5.
[30] *Jour.* III, 474-5.
[31] *Jour.* VII, 160.
[32] *Letters, etc.: Poetry and Imagination, Transcendency*, 72.
[33] Ibid.

Dante, one would say, did the same thing before he wrote the verses."[34] Following the same principle, Shakspeare, the ideal dramatist, makes his characters and their speeches as lifelike, as realistic, as if they were possible human beings. This is true even of Ariel, Caliban, and the fairies in the Midsummer Night's Dream. The "force of representation so plants his figures before him that he treats them as real; talks to them as if they were bodily there; puts words in their mouth such as they would have spoken, and is affected by them as by persons. . . . The humor of Falstaff, the terror of Macbeth, have each their swarm of fit thoughts and images, as if Shakspeare had known and reported the men, instead of inventing them at his desk."[35]

The satisfaction to be derived from such objectifying of the imaginative is of the same general character as that which attends everywhere the achievement of adequate expression. The same requirements of precision have to be met in even greater measure perhaps in the writing which has as its purpose definition, whether of the earthly or spiritual. Emerson finds definition truly successful only when it makes evident the relationship between the particular fact or facts under consideration and the general law which affects them; when it shows the intellectual or spiritual in the physical; the One in the Many. The lawyer or judge is most to be commended who disregards technical points and draws the true distinctions which "come from and . . . go to the sound human understanding"; which have the "merit of common sense . . . the same quality we admire in Aristotle, Montaigne, Cervantes, or in Samuel Johnson, or Franklin."[36] On the higher levels, definition is philosophy. In this regard, Plato surpasses all previous philosophers. He, by recognizing the cardinal principles of Unity and Variety, has a complete insight which brings order out of the previous crudities of conception regarding nature and morals.[37] In the same way, Coleridge is superior to Landor. Landor, Emerson says, "is a man full of thoughts, but not, like Coleridge, a man of ideas. Only from a mind conversant with the First Philosophy can definitions be expected. Coleridge has contributed many valuable ones to modern literature. Mr. Landor's definitions are only enumerations of particulars; the generic law is not seized."[38]

Emerson's own success in definition is considerable. Partly as the result of his ability to look at things either from the Yankee or the Platonic angle, his exposition of philosophical ideas, especially those of opposing

[34] *Natural History of Intellect: Powers and Laws of Thought*, 49.

[35] *Letters, etc.: Poetry and Imagination, Creation*, 43–4.

[36] *Society and Solitude: Eloquence*, 88.

[37] *Representative Men: Plato*, 45–54.

[38] *Natural History of Intellect: Walter Savage Landor*, 346.

points of view, is admirable in its fair-mindedness and its lucidity. On some occasions, it is true, he admits his own inadequacy to find words to express his conceptions: as in the essay on *The Over-Soul*,[39] or in that on *Civilization*.[40] But in the field of human relationships, what could be more discerning than his lecture on *The Conservative*,[41] with its evenly sustained debate between the standpatter and the progressive? And with similar success in metaphysical regions is his lecture on *The Transcendentalist*.[42]

Thus in theory and practice Emerson displays his belief that "Skill in writing consists in making every word cover a thing."[43] It makes no difference whether the thing be seen with the eye of sense, or the eye of vision, whether the writing be prose or poetry, whether it be essay, speech, drama, or philosophy, precision is essential. There is, it is true, a difference in the kind of accuracy demanded: each thing being accurate after its kind, according to whether it is material or ideal. The actual must be so closely described as to accord with the impressions of sense. And the ideal must not only be represented in fit symbols, but has to satisfy the additional requirement that it be as concrete an embodiment as if it were an object of the senses.

b. The Word and the Thing

The next main problem raised by the Emersonian demand for adequacy in expression is this: If every word should cover a thing, what is the thing? Is it the mental process, or is it the natural and physical fact which gives body to the thought? Is it the thought or the object of thought? Does expression represent the writer's intellectual operations or the experience and observation of Nature which furnish the material for these operations? Emerson is not always careful to distinguish; and sometimes he means one, sometimes the other. He says that Shakspeare "could say the thing finer, nearer to the purity of thought itself than any other";[44] and, on the other hand, writes: "Language clothes Nature, as the air clothes the earth, taking the exact form and pressure of every object."[45] The first conception, that of mental reproduction, is most frequent when Emerson is thinking of the individual mind as a part of the Universal Mind or Over-Soul. The second conception, equating style with Nature, appears usually when Emerson has in mind the doctrine that Nature is the symbolic expression of spirit. That the two conceptions may easily run into one

[39] *Essays* I, 269–70.

[40] *Society and Solitude*, 19.

[41] *Nature, etc.*

[42] *Nature, etc.*

[43] *Jour.* IV, 326.

[44] *Jour.* X, 29.

[45] *Jour.* IV, 146.

another is hereby evident. For there is no great difficulty in thinking of Nature, the means by which the Divine Spirit or Over-Soul finds expression, as having the same meaning as the Over-Soul; as being, at least for the purposes of expression, identical with it.

Not only do the two conceptions converge in this way, but whatever discrepancy there may be between them is apparently resolvable. Emerson's explanation involves a discussion of a psychological process which is inclusive of one we have already discussed in detail, in the section on the *Symbol*. This is the process by which the writer may be able to have at his command the proper kind of symbols. The writer's success in the expression of the ideal, we saw, comes about through his having the kind of experience that will make, at the proper hour, adequate symbols arise in his mind to cover the thought; and this experience, we discovered, is life of congruous simplicity in natural surroundings. Similarly, at the beginning of his essay on Goethe in *Representative Men*, Emerson declares that all writing, not only the symbolic, but writing in general, is the result of a fusion of the material and the mental, accompanied by an individual process of selection. "I find a provision in the constitution of the world," he says, "for the writer, or secretary, who is to report the doings of the miraculous spirit of life that everywhere throbs and works. His office is a reception of the facts into the mind, and then a selection of the eminent and characteristic experiences. . . . The memory is a kind of looking-glass, which, having received the images of surrounding objects, is touched with life, and disposes them in a new order. The facts do not lie in it inert; but some subside and others shine; so that we soon have a new picture, composed of the eminent experiences."

Thus the individual mind garners from experience and Nature, sifts, and shapes into expression. In Emerson's discussion of style, however, the combination of the operations is not always prominent. Sometimes he emphasizes style as a copy of mind; at other times he lays stress on style as a copy of Nature.

He often deals wholly with the intellectual product, and disregards the preparatory steps, regarding expression as a photograph of the writer's mind. He tells us, for instance, that in conversation with his brother Charles he "maintained that the Lycidas was a copy from the poet's mind printed out in the book, notwithstanding all the mechanical difficulties, as clear and wild as it had shone at first in the sky of his own thought."[46]

Evidently *Lycidas*, in Emerson's opinion, is the product of the higher and nobler part of Milton's mind, the Reason, the individual's share of the World Soul. And indeed, expression is truly adequate only when the writer's mind is submitted to and a part of the Divine Mind or Over-Soul, for then the objects of Nature speak to him in their true sense as symbols.

[46] *Jour.* III, 571.

"The condition of true naming, on the poet's part, is his resigning himself to the divine *aura* which breathes through forms, and accompanying that." When the mind is thus in unison with the Universal Spirit, "his speech is thunder, his thought is law, and his words are universally intelligible as the plants and animals." At such times intensity is necessary to accuracy. "The poet knows that he speaks adequately . . . only when he speaks somewhat wildly, or with the 'flower of the Mind.' "[47] Emerson's highest wish in regard to expression is uttered in the quatrain:

O Hafiz, give me thought—
In fiery figures cast,
For all beside is naught,
All else is din and blast.[48]

And in the lines:

Give me of the true,—
Whose ample leaves and tendrils curled
Among the silver hills of heaven
Draw everlasting dew;
Wine of wine,
Blood of the world,
Form of forms, and mould of statures,
That I intoxicated,
And by the draught assimilated,
May float at pleasure through all natures;
The bird-language rightly spell,
And that which roses say so well.[49]

It is clear, then, that words become one with mental things in the loftiest sense when the mental actions represented are themselves elevated. Emerson himself secured what he believed to be exact expression by his method of setting down the results of his own communings with the divine spirit. Late in life he wrote in his *Journals:* "I am so purely a spectator that I have absolute confidence that all pure spectators will agree with me, whenever I make a careful report. I told Alcott that every one of my expressions concerning 'God,' or the 'soul,' etc., is entitled to attention as testimony, because it is independent, not calculated, not part of any system, but spontaneous, and the nearest word I could find to the thing."[50] Emerson's success as an auditor of the spiritual is revealed in many shorter passages in his writings; it appears at length most notably in just those essays where we should expect to find it: those on *The Over-Soul* and *Spiritual Laws*.[51]

[47] *Essays* II: *The Poet*, 26–7.
[48] *Jour.* IX, 75.
[49] *Poems: Bacchus*, 125–6.
[50] *Jour.* X, 191.
[51] *Essays* I.

The connection between the Over-Soul and adequacy in expression extends to include two important corollaries. The first is the classification of literature into what Emerson calls primary and secondary. The other is the recognition of the fact that there are some expressions which because of their relationship to the Over-Soul or outgrowth from it, are ultimate phrasings of divine truth, not to be improved upon.

Writing which issues intimately from the promptings of the Over-Soul which is inspired, is nearer the truth than mere reflections of other men's inspiration. Emerson classifies literature as primary or secondary. Primary literature includes all the sacred books or bibles of the world; all writing in which the spiritual and the symbolic are combined anew without reference to similar literature in the past. "The old Psalms and Gospels are mighty as ever; showing that what people call religion is literature; that is to say,—here was one who knew how to put his statement, and it stands forever, and people feel its truth, as he did, and say, *Thus said the Lord*, whilst it is only that he had the true literary genius, which they fancy they despise."[52] Primary literature includes also Dante's *Vita Nuova*, which, Emerson says, "reads like the book of Genesis, as if written before literature, whilst truth yet existed. . . . It is the Bible of Love."[53] On the other hand, such a writer as Shelley, though his ideas are Platonic, is not newly and independently conscious of these ideas; he writes secondarily. Harsh comment has been made regarding Emerson's critical ability because of his failure to appreciate Shelley; and it seems surprising that with such community of belief there should not have been more sympathy on Emerson's part. The explanation lies in his conviction of the secondariness of Shelley's poems: "Shelley," he says, "is never a poet. His mind is uniformly imitative; all his poems composite. A fine English scholar he is, with taste, ear, and memory; but imagination, the original authentic fire of the bard, he has not. He is clearly modern, and shares with Wordsworth and Coleridge, Byron, and Hemans the feeling of the Infinite, which so labors for expression in their different genius. But all his lines are arbitrary, not necessary, and therefore, though evidently a devout and brave man, I can never read his verses."[54]

Imitation is to be avoided, but there are some words which we cannot and should not wish to do without, though they have been used for ages. Such words are philosophical or sacred in import; they are the expressions of the common sense of mankind regarding its knowledge of the Over-Soul. Emerson is fond of Coleridge's statement, "Language thinks for us." Carlyle, he says, has added nothing to the meaning already crystallized in the word *hero*.[55] In the most common words is packed the philosophical

[52] *Jour*. IX, 345. Compare the distinction between primary and second words in Plato's *Cratylus*.

[53] *Jour*. VI, 418.

[54] *Jour*. V, 344.

[55] *Jour*. VIII, 123.

and religious wisdom of the centuries, so that "After a man has made great progress, and has come, as he fancies, to heights hitherto unscaled, the common words still fit his thought; nay, he only now finds for the first time how wise they were;— . . . *Reason*, *Conscience*, *Substance*, *Accidence*, *Nature*, *Relation*, *Fortune*, *Fate*, *Genius*, *Element*, *Person*;—'twill be long before he needs a new coat. . . . After the student has wasted all night speculating on his analogies and ties to the world and to the starry heaven, the first words he meets in the morning book are *microcosm*, *macrocosm*."

And if these are "tools provided by the Genius of Humanity"[56] for the use of the philosopher, the religious writer is likewise indebted. Emerson acknowledges the debt thus: "Iamblichus in answer to the query, 'Why of significant names we prefer such as are barbaric to our own?' says, among other reasons: 'Barbarous names have much emphasis, greater conciseness, and less ambiguity, variety, and multitude'; and then afterwards: 'But the Barbarians are stable in their manners, and firmly continue to employ the same words. Hence they are dear to the gods, and proffer words which are grateful to them.' . . . Now the words 'God,' 'Grace,' 'Prayer,' 'Heaven,' 'Hell,' are these barbarous and sacred words, to which we must still return, whenever we would speak an ecstatic and universal sense? There are objections to them, no doubt, for academical use, but when the professor's gown is taken off, Man will come back to them."[57]

For the same reason as he respects single words in which adequate expression has once and for all been arrived at, Emerson holds proverbs in high regard. They are likewise "the literature of reason, or the statements of an absolute truth without qualification,"[58] so that "In any controversy concerning morals, an appeal may be made with safety to the sentiments which the language of the people expresses. Proverbs, words and grammar-inflections convey the public sense with more purity and precision than the wisest individual."[59] Of the same value are those passages from the masters of literature which because of their wise precision and universality are, as Emerson says of Shakspeare, "pulverized into proverbs, and dispersed into human discourse."[60] The relation of proverbs and other idiomatic language to the problems of style requires fuller discussion elsewhere; here it is desirable merely to point out its connection with Emerson's conception of style as a reflection of the author's mind when it partakes of the qualities of the Universal Mind or Over-Soul.

[56] *Jour.* VIII, 17.

[57] *Jour.* VI, 127-8.

[58] *Essays* I: *Compensation*, 108–9.

[59] *Essays* II: *Nominalist and Realist*, 230–1.

[60] *Jour.* VIII, 39.

Thus Emerson, in speaking of style, stresses its mental origin, especially when the relation of expression to the Over-Soul is involved. But just as he sometimes disregards the material with which mind works, so, on the other hand, he may set aside, for the time, the mental operations and concentrate his attention on that which furnishes the substance of thought—Experience or Nature. His belief that style should mirror experience Emerson makes clear when he interprets with reference to style his wife's dream of a statue, "the speech of which was not quite speech either, but something better, which seemed at last identical with the thing itself spoken of. It described . . . life and being;—and then, by a few slight movements of the head and body, it gave the most forcible picture of death and decay and corruption, and then became all radiant again with the signs of resurrection. I thought it a just description of that Eloquence to which we are all entitled—are we not?—which shall be no idle tale, but the suffering of the action, and the action it describes."[61]

And as with Experience, so also with Nature, when that furnishes the subject-matter. Wordsworth, says Emerson, "has writ lines that are like outward nature, so fresh, so simple, so durable."[62] And even closer parallelism of feature may be desirable. In descriptions of nature, the author is required to make almost a tracing of that which he is picturing. We find in the Journals: "The descriptive talent in the poet seems to depend on a certain lakelike passiveness to receive the picture of the whole landscape in its native proportions, uninjured, and then with sweet heedfulness the caution of love, to transfer it to the tablet of language."[64] Again Emerson writes: "I should like . . . to have water-color tried in the art of writing. Let our troubadours have one of these Spanish slopes of the dry ponds or basins which run from Walden to the river at Fairhaven, in this September dress of color, under this glowering sky,—the Walden Sierras in September, given as a theme, and they required to daguerreotype that in good words."[64]

Such comparisons between drawing or painting and writing as are made in these two passages are frequent in Emerson, partly, of course, as the result of their common use as mediums of expression. Two other reasons for their occurrence are more peculiarly Emersonian.

He believes, as we have seen, that each small law holds universally; and hence is pleased to show that the laws of one art apply to another. Emerson manifests no concern over the confusion of the genres; he is governed not by the *Laokoon*, but by the doctrine of Each and All. Under the heading Ἓν καὶ πᾶν he writes in his Journal: "An intelligent painter, for

[61] *Jour.* VI, 129-30.
[62] *Jour.* II, 402.
[63] *Jour.* VI, 361.
[64] *Jour.* VII, 505.

example, cannot give rules for his art, or suggest hints for the direction or correction of his scholar, without saying what is pertinent and true to a far greater extent than the circle of painting; e.g., 'No great painter is nice in pencils'; '*Nulla dies sine linea.*' "[65]

The other reason, which relates directly to our present subject of style as an immediate copy of Nature, is that a word-painting of Nature has a similar effect to that of Nature itself. Since Nature is the expression of spirit, it is a riddle, constantly hinting at its solution, always revealing partial answers, but never giving up its complete secret. And a word-facsimile of Nature, a verbal landscape painting, affords similar tantalizing glimpses.

Nature, in Emerson's view, is a mysterious book, always open, yet intelligible only on occasion. Even when its message cannot be read, it fascinates. "Every object in Nature," Emerson says, "is a word to signify some fact in the mind. But when that fact is not yet put into English words, when I look at the tree or the river and have not yet definitely made out what they would say to me, they are by no means unimpressive. I wait for them, I enjoy them before they yet speak. I feel as if I stood by an ambassador charged with the message of his king, which he does not deliver because the hour when he should say it has not yet arrived."[66] I "feel," he says in another passage, "that every one of those remarkable effects in landscape which occasionally catch and delight the eye, as, for example, a long vista in the woods, trees on the shore of a lake coming quite down to the water, a long reach in a river, a double or triple row of uplands or mountains seen one over the other . . . must be the rhetoric of some thought not yet detached for the conscious intellect."[67] Such "dim anticipation of profound meaning"[68] explains the love of nature. "What is that," asks Emerson, "but the presentiment of intelligence of it? Nature preparing to be a language to us?"[69]

Thus Nature is a cipher always hinting at its true solution; it is always just ready to pull aside the curtain which separates the human from the divine. Therefore a literal transcription of parts of Nature into language will suggest a spiritual meaning, even if it does not declare it directly. Of interest, accordingly, in connection with Emerson's conception of style as a copy of Nature is his joy in the mere names of natural objects, not because of what they signify but because of what they intimate. And it is important, too, that as a consequence of his pleasure in such intimations, he finds value in poetry which consists of nothing more esoteric than a list of natural objects accurately described.

[65] *Jour.* IV, 26.
[66] *Natural History of Intellect: Powers and Laws of Thought*, 5–6.
[67] *Jour.* V, 470-1.
[68] *Jour.* V, 76.
[69] *Jour.* V, 510.

Emerson takes a delight in British place-names no less keen though more philosophically motivated than that which has inspired the modern philologist to delve into their origins: "The names are excellent,—an atmosphere of legendary melody spread over the land. Older than all epics and histories which clothe a nation, this undershirt sits close to the body. What history too, and what stores of primitive and savage observation it infolds . . . . Waltham is strong town; Radcliffe is red cliff; and so on:—a sincerity and use in naming very striking to an American, whose country is whitewashed all over by unmeaning names, the cast-off clothes of the country from which its emigrants came; or named at a pinch from a psalm-tune. But the English are those 'barbarians' of Jamblichus, who 'are stable in their manners, and firmly continue to employ the same words, which also are dear to the gods.' "[70]

Botanical names also have their charms. In *Concord Walks*,[71] Emerson recommends an arboretum of trees and plants which have legendary, biblical, or historical associations, such as the upas, asphodel, nepenthe, haemony, moly, spikenard, and lotus.[72] But the poetry in such names may be much more indirect. Emerson finds charm even in apparently so technical a treatise as the *Report of Herbaceous Plants in Massachusetts*. For "the mere names of reeds and grasses, of the milkweeds, of the mint tribe and the gentians, of mallows and trefoils," bring up images, and "the names are poems often. *Erigeron*, because it grows old early, is thus named the Old Man of the Spring. . . . The Plantain (Plantago Major) . . . is called by the Indians 'White Man's Foot.' . . . The naming of the localities comforts us—'ponds,' 'shady roads,' 'sandy woods,' 'wet pastures,' etc. I begin to see the sun and moon, and to share the life of Nature, as under the spell of the sweetest pastoral Poet."[73]

And in fact poetry itself may be composed of similar constituents. "Thus Thomson's Seasons and the best parts of many old and many new poets are simply enumerations by a person who felt the beauty of the common sights and sounds, without any attempt to draw a moral or affix a meaning."[74]

As Emerson regards expression, then, it is adequate if it is an accurate record of thought; or of the substance of the thought, Nature and Experience; or in case the two are properly combined through the activity and selectiveness of the individual intelligence. Whichever it may be, it gains in worth if it is spiritual in character, either as a result of the individual Reason's communion with the Over-Soul, or through the symbolic character of Nature—even when the ideal truth symbolized is but vaguely suggested.

[70] *English Traits: Aristocracy*, 179.

[71] *Natural History of Intellect*, 174.

[72] See also *Jour.* VI, 24.

[73] *Jour.* VI, 193-4.

[74] *Letters, etc.: Poetry and Imagination, Imagination*, 22–3.

c. Limitations

So far the requirements of adequacy in expression involve a pertinacious heed to accuracy in describing both the material and the ideal; and an earnest attempt at exact rendering of either the mental, or the material, or the fusion of the twain. Such complexity and uncertainty of aim as these stylistic conceptions must cause is sufficient in itself to indicate the limitations of language as a medium of communication. That these exist is indeed pointed at obviously enough by the fact that poetry may satisfy even if composed of an unadorned series of natural phenomena accurately depicted.

Emerson craves adequacy; the word and thing should be one. And yet he recognizes that for several reasons words are ineffective means of utterance. In the first place, language is restricted in capacity; words are inherently far distant from things. In the second place, some things which language tries to convey it is not meet that human beings should be potent to phrase; anything partaking of the Spirit, including Nature, its method of expression, is, in major degree, ineffable. In the third place, shortcomings may develop from the writer's own weakness; he may be unable to compass that combination of elevation and submission which marks the unity of the individual mind with the Over-Soul, and as a result the time or the literary point of view may enter to invalidate the purity of his writing.

Language is intrinsically defective. It is not a direct mode of conveying thought. It describes, rather than *is* the thing. And it is this only when it is successful; more often it merely suggests. "As Boscovich taught that two particles of matter never touch, so it seems true that nothing can be described as it is. The most accurate picture is only symbols and suggestions of the thing, but from the nature of language all remote."[75] "We learn with joy and wonder this new and flattering art of language. deceived by the exhilaration which accompanies the attainment of each new word. We fancy we gain somewhat. We gain nothing. It seemed to men that words come nearer to the thing; described the fact; were the fact. They learned later that they only suggest it. It is an operose, circuitous way of putting us in mind of the thing,—of flagellating our attention."[76]

It is interesting that when Emerson conveyed to Carlyle his sense of the feebleness of language, Carlyle replied in entire agreement: "What you say about the vast *imperfection* of all modes of utterance is most true indeed. Let a man speak and sing, and do, and sputter and gesticulate as he may,—the meaning of him is most ineffectually shown forth, poor fellow; rather *indicated* as if by straggling symbols, than *spoken* or visually expressed! Poor fellow!"[77]

[75] *Jour.* IV, 266.
[76] *Jour.* VI, 274-5.
[77] *C. E. Corr.* II, 96.

Thus language suffers from a general incompetence. Further particular difficulties beset it. "There are many things that refuse to be recorded,—perhaps the larger half."[78] These things are spiritual. When Emerson speaks of Spirit, of the Over-Soul, even of Character, he almost invariably includes a word concerning the difficulty of saying anything exact about the subject. "Of that ineffable essence which we call Spirit," he writes, "he that thinks most, will say least. We can foresee God in the coarse, and, as it were, distant phenomena of matter; but when we try to define and describe himself, both language and thought desert us, and we are as helpless as fools and savages."[79] Of the Over-Soul, he declares: "Language cannot paint it with his colors. It is too subtile."[80] In a letter to a Quaker friend, he wrote: "For the science of God our language is unexpressive and merely prattle: we need simpler and universal signs, as algebra compared with arithmetic. . . . And when we have heaped up a mountain of speeches, we have still to begin again, having nowise expressed the simple unalterable fact."[81] Of theism he writes in his *Journals:* "Here we feel at once that we have no language; that words are only auxiliary and not adequate, are suggestions and not copies of our cogitation."[82] And even when the human and divine meet, as in life and character, he feels no greater certainty of achievement. Of "this omnipresent riddle of life," he writes: "Nobody can state it. Speech pants after it in vain; all poetry, all philosophy in their parts, or entire, never express it, though that is still their aim; they only approximate. Nobody can say what everybody feels, and what all would jump to hear, if it should be said, and, moreover, which all have a confused belief *might be* said."[83] And concerning the comparatively unmysterious element called character, he admits modestly: "We are painting the lightning with charcoal."[84]

Not only is Emerson troubled by the inefficiency of language in describing God and his attributes, but he is aware of its difficulty in reaching that degree of intensity of expression which betokens true union with the divine. Doubtfully he inquires: "Do you think ecstasy is ever communicable?"[85] And in another mystical passage in his *Journals*, he reflects: "I think that he only is rightly immortal to whom all things are immortal; he who witnesses personally the creation of the world; he who enunciates profoundly the names of Pan, of Jove, of Pallas, of Bacchus, of Proteus, of Baal, of Ahriman, of Hari, of Satan, of Hell, of Nemesis, of

[78] *Jour.* III, 492.
[79] *Nature, etc.: Spirit,* 61–2.
[80] *Essays* I: *The Over-Soul*, 271.
[81] *Representative Men*, 316-7.
[82] *Jour.* IV, 416.
[83] *Jour.* IV, 29.
[84] *Essays* II: *Character*, 104.
[85] *Jour.* VII, 522.

the Furies, of Odin, and of Hertha;—knowing well the need he has of these, and a far richer vocabulary; knowing well how imperfect and insufficient to his needs language is: requiring music, requiring dancing, as languages; a dance, for example, that shall sensibly express our astronomy, our solar system, and seasons, in its course."[86]

Not only the Divine, but Nature, itself the language of spirit, is also too sacred in character to be wholly paralleled in words. "Nature will outwit the wisest writer, though it were Plato or Spinoza, and his book will fall into this dead limbo we call literature; else the writer were God, too, and his work another nature."[87] At the beginning of his lecture on *The Method of Nature*,[88] Emerson says that the subject is one in which "we must necessarily appeal to the intuition, and aim much more to suggest than to describe." We have seen that Emerson wishes the writer to paint Nature accurately and thereby obtain insight into the Spiritual. The difficulty of so doing, however, he expresses frequently. "The word can never cover the thing. You don't expect to describe a sunrise."[89] He speaks of "the live repose which that amphitheatre of a valley behind Ball's Hill reflects to my eye, and which Homer or Shakspeare could not re-form for me in words."[90] Both despair and hope appear in his *Journal* record: "As I looked at some wild, tall trees this afternoon, I felt that Nature was still inaccessible; that, for all the fine poems that have been written, the word is not yet spoken that can cover the charm of morning or evening or woods or lakes, and to-morrow something may be uttered better than any strain of Pindar or Shakspear."[91] The poem *My Garden*[92] is chiefly an expression of this thought. In another poem, *The World-Soul*, occur the lines,

We cannot learn the cipher
  That's writ upon our cell;
Stars taunt us by a mystery
  Which we could never spell.[93]

Because of their divine character, language is thus incapable of representing Spirit, or Nature, the expression of Spirit. Another handicap which it encounters is their "infinite diffuseness.'[94] "What baulks all language is the broad, radiating, immensely distributive action of Nature or spirit. If it were linear, if it were successive, step by step, jet after jet,

[86] *Jour.* VII, 228.
[87] *Jour.* VI, 550.
[88] *Nature, etc.*, 198.
[89] *Jour.* III, 286.
[90] *Jour.* III, 418.
[91] *Jour.* IV, 145.
[92] *Poems*, 229–231.
[93] *Poems*, 17.
[94] *Jour.* VI, 65.

like our small human agency, we could follow it with language; but it mocks us."[95] In conviction of weakness, Emerson exclaims: "Can you hear what the morning says to you, and believe *that?* Can you bring home the summits of Wachusett, Greylock, and the New Hampshire hills? the Savin groves of Middlesex? the sedgy ripples of the old Colony ponds? the sunny shores of your own bay, and the low Indian hills of Rhode Island? the savageness of pine-woods? Can you bottle the efflux of a June noon, and bring home the tops of Uncanoonuc? The landscape is vast, complete, alive. We step about, dibble and dot, and attempt in poor linear ways to hobble after those angelic radiations."[96]

Thus adequacy of utterance may be hindered or rendered impossible through the inefficiency of language as a medium. It is inherently indirect; and it is a human instrument, unfitted for description of the divine. There are other obstacles to expression which have much more to do with the writer than with his tools. For one thing, the character of the writer's mind has a good deal to do with his power of achievement; this has been evident in all that has been said of the relation of style to the Over-Soul. Exaltation of the individual intelligence and surrender to the World Spirit are indispensable to the writer who is trying to represent divine thought, and the lack thereof will damage or nullify the effect of his writing. "I dare not speak for it," says Emerson in his essay on the Over-Soul. "My words do not carry its august sense; they fall short and cold. Only itself can inspire whom it will."[97]

Completeness of submission to the divine voice alone can bring about adequate expression. But utter obedience and hence entire success are often prevented by two other forces: the time and the literary point of view.

Fidelity to the fact is difficult because the spirit of the age is always intruding. "We sit down with intent to write truly, and end with making a book that contains no thought of ours, but merely the tune of the time. Here I am writing a ΦBK poem, free to say what I choose, and it looks to me now as if it would scarce express thought of mine, but be a sort of *fata morgana* reflecting the images of Byron, Shakespear, and the newspapers."[98] "As no air-pump can by any means make a perfect vacuum, so neither can any artist entirely exclude the conventional, the local, the perishable from his book, or write a book of pure thought, that shall be as efficient, in all respects, to a remote posterity, as to contemporaries, or rather to the second age. Each age, it is found, must write its own books; or rather, each generation for the next succeeding."[99]

[95] *Jour.* IX, 114.
[96] *Natural History of Intellect: Country Life*, 157.
[97] *Essays* I, 269–70.
[98] *Jour.* III, 333.
[99] *Nature, etc.: The American Scholar*, 88.

The interference which the literary point of view entails, Emerson explains as derived from the inferiority of the writing process to the thought which it is trying to reproduce. The thought partakes of the nature of Reason, being uncalculated and natural. The writing process is for practical ends, and is of the Understanding, artificial and carefully contrived. Emerson thus relates the complexities of the situation: "How hard to write the truth. 'Let a man rejoice in the truth, and not that he has found it,' said my early oracle.[100] Well, so soon as I have seen the truth I clap my hands and rejoice, and go back to see it and forward to tell men. I am so pleased therewith that presently it vanishes. Then am I submiss, and it appears 'without observation.' I write it down, and it is gone. Yet is the benefit of others and their love of receiving truth from me the reason of my interest and effort to obtain it, and thus do I double and treble with God. The Reason refuses to play at couples with Understanding; to subserve the private ends of the understanding."[101]

To the same purport, though transcendental terms are laid aside on this occasion, Emerson writes: "What mischief is in this art of writing. An unlettered man considers a fact, to learn what it means; the lettered man does not sooner see it than it occurs to him how it can be told. And this fact of looking at it as an artist blinds him to the better half of the fact. Unhappily he is conscious of the misfortune, which rather makes it worse. As cultivated flowers turn their stamens to petals, so does he turn the practick part to idle show. He has a morbid growth of eyes; he sees with his feet."[102] The critic especially is thus hampered. "The most important difference in criticism is whether one writes from life, or from a literary point of view. 'Tis difficult for a writer not to be bookish and conventional. If he writes from manly experience and feeling, his page is a power."[103]

Emerson makes strenuous demands on the writer. Words should fit the thing, should cover the thing, should be one with things. The writer cannot rest easy if he does not describe the material fact precisely; he must also hold himself to the highest possible standards of exact adjustment when he describes spiritualities. He strives for expression which proceeds directly from, and reflects, a judiciously arrived-at union of the physical and the mental; though often he is less interested in the amalgamation than in copying either the mental operations or Nature itself.

Yet at the same time achievement of these desiderata is in many ways impossible. Emerson agrees with his Swedenborgian friend, Sampson Reed, that it is only in heaven that words become one with things.[104]

[100] His aunt, Mary Moody Emerson.

[101] *Jour.* IV, 74-5.

[102] *Jour.* III, 332.

[103] *Jour.* IX, 281.

[104] *Jour.* III, 492.

Earthly language is a roundabout way of getting at the thing; it is, furthermore, because of its terrene character, unsuited to the expression of the heavenly, even when, as in Nature, it is but partly divulged. It is not the thing, but a suggestion, an approximation of it. And as if these were not enough hindrances to adequacy, the writer's spiritual insight may be deficient; he is, whatever his aspirations to declare eternal laws, to a considerable extent a creature of time and circumstance; and he may be diverted from the truth by the very fact that he is a writer.

As Gilbert has it in the *Mikado*, "Here's a howdy-do!" What is the author to do? He has been spurred on to intense effort, and then, in the midst of it, he is assured that it is all to no end. So far as it goes, the way out of his predicament is simple: Attempt the impossible. It should be the *aim* of language, at least, "to describe the fact, and not merely suggest it. If you, with these sketchers and *dilettanti*, give me some conscious, indeterminate compound word, it is like a daub of color to hide the defects of your drawing. Sharper sight would see and indicate the true line. The poet both draws well, and colors at the same time."[105] "Our aim in our writings ought to be to make daylight shine through them."[106]

The writer "counts it all nonsense that they say, that some things are undescribable. He believes that all that can be thought can be written, first or last; and he would report the Holy Ghost, or attempt it. Nothing so broad, so subtle, or so dear, but comes therefore commended for his pen, and he will write. In his eyes, a man is the faculty of reporting, and the universe is the possibility of being reported. . . . Whatever can be thought can be spoken, and still rises for utterance, though to rude and stammering organs. If they cannot compass it, it [Nature] waits and works, until, at last, it moulds them to its perfect will and is articulated."[107]

Emerson's attitude toward adequacy in expression, not only in theory but also in practice, is one of mingled determination and realization of impossibility. He frequently acknowledges incapacity; and yet goes on to try just the same. This is especially characteristic of the essays in which he speaks of the difficulty or defeat encountered in describing the Divine, and Nature, its outward reflection. He confesses his inability to express his feeling about the Over-Soul, and writes perhaps his noblest essay. He declares in conviction of futility: "If you wish to know the shortcomings of poetry and language, try to reproduce the October picture to a city company."[108] Yet that he creates the Indian Summer perfectly his second essay on Nature testifies.[109] And there are other

[105] *Jour.* VI, 215.
[106] *Jour.* V, 198.
[107] *Representative Men: Goethe*, 262–3.
[108] *Natural History of Intellect: Country Life*, 156.
[109] *Essays* II, 169–70.

examples of his close attainment to what he declares cannot be, in *Spiritual Laws*,[110] in *Works and Days*,[111] and in the first essay on *Nature*.[112] The following lines from *My Garden*[113] sum up his problem, his failure, and his success:

> Wandering voices in the air
>   And murmurs in the wold
> Speak what I cannot declare,
>   Yet cannot all withhold.

If Emerson recognizes the partial quality of his own success, and is conscious of the difficulties of expression for all writers, he does not, on that account, lose his optimism. He writes to Carlyle: "Burns might have added a better verse to his poem, importing that one might write Iliads or Hamlets, and yet come short of truth by infinity, as every written word must; but 'the man's the gowd for a' that.' "[114] And though so far as he is himself concerned he tells Carlyle that he is "certain and content that the truth can very well spare me, and have itself spoken by another without leaving it or me the worse," he is bold enough to write also: "My faith in the Writers, as an organic class, increases daily, and in the possibility to a faithful man of arriving at statements for which he shall not feel responsible, but which shall be parallel with nature."[115]

2. Each and All

Belief in the symbol as the ideal form of expression cooperates with and includes another doctrine prominent in Emerson's collection—that of Each and All, as he most frequently describes it, or the One and the Many, to use its Platonic and more usual name. This involves the conception that any natural or spiritual law, or the whole of Nature or of Spirit, is discoverable, realizable, and predicable through proper understanding of any single object in Nature. Each little drop of water includes and typifies all that is knowable of the mighty ocean; each grain of sand wholly represents the pleasant land. Furthermore, since everything in Nature is the expression of Spirit, either drop or grain is a complete conveyor of Divine Truth. Everything in Nature affords the basis for earthly or spiritual generalization. All is in each.

The application of this theory to art and to literature is not difficult; and when once applied it has extensive consequences. These radiate from the point at which the doctrine of Each and All meets the belief in the Symbol. The purpose of every art, so Emerson believes, is to represent

[110] *Essays* I.
[111] *Society and Solitude.*
[112] *Nature, etc.*
[113] *Poems*, 231.
[114] *C. E. Corr.* I, 121-2.
[115] *C. E. Corr*, II, 58-9.

the One, or Spirit, as the Reason, the higher part of the intelligence, perceives it. But this ideal One can be expressed only through the Many, the objects of Nature and experience; the material affords an indirect, but the sole means of conveying the eternal Unity. Thus in writing, the symbol, by which the ideal is expressed under a variety of material forms, makes the expression of Identity possible.

To the mutability of the Many in the service of communicating the One, Emerson admits no exceptions. "The metamorphosis of Nature," he says, "shows itself in nothing more than this, that there is no word in our language that cannot become typical to us of Nature by giving it emphasis. The world is a Dancer; it is a Rosary; it is a Torrent; it is a Boat; a Mist; a Spider's Snare; it is what you will; and the metaphor will hold, and it will give the imagination keen pleasure. Swifter than light the world converts itself into that thing you name, and all things find their right place under this new and capricious classification."[116]

This infinite dilation to which every object may be subjected has the effect of making every symbol suggestive of the universal Identity. Even though the writer's purpose is but to find a particular material expression for his particular ideal thought, without any conscious attempt to typify the pervading oneness of Spirit, the symbol has a haunting charm arising from its intimation that since this thing is interchangeable for that, the cause of the convertibility must be a comprehensive Unity. And here indeed is the origin of figures of speech. "Metonymy," writes Emerson in his *Journals*, "seems to begin in the slightest change of name, or, detecting identity under variety of surface. Boys please themselves with crying to the coachman, 'Put on the string,' instead of *lash*. With calling a fire-engine a *tub;* and the engine men *Tigers*. A boy's game of ball is called *Four Old Cats*. Poetry calls a snake a *worm*. In a shipwreck, the sea novel finds '*cordilleras* of water.'" One more example, particularly pleasing to the idealist, "I can never lose the ludicrous effect of using the word *tin* for *money*."[117]

Every symbol, therefore, expresses both a particular and a universal truth; and thus the theories of Each and All and of the Symbol are, strictly speaking, inseparable.

To the theory of Each and All as well as to Emerson's Yankee common sense is to be attributed his success in avoiding the error into which more mystic and less poetical idealists have fallen in their use of the symbol. This is the fallacy of assuming a rigid correspondence between Nature and Spirit, part for part, as if any one form could be used symbolically in just one fixed way. Emerson deplores especially Swedenborg's theological tendency to see one absolutely set equation of meaning between the

[116] *Jour.* VI, 18.
[117] *Jour.* VIII, 296-7.

natural and the divine: "The slippery Proteus in not so easily caught. In nature, each individual symbol plays innumerable parts, as each particle of matter circulates in turn through every system. The central identity enables any one symbol to express successively all the qualities and shades of real being. In the transmission of the heavenly waters, every hose fits every hydrant."[118]

The consequences of this belief on Emerson's style deserve specific notice. Having found an individual symbol, which some moment's inspiration has consecrated, he feels perfectly free to use it later in application to something quite different. When the poet has interpreted natural objects in one way, Emerson says, he does not "rest in this meaning, but he makes the same objects exponents of his next thought."[119]

So in *Civilization*,[120] after Emerson has spoken of the mechanical advantages man has gained by harnessing the elements, and has said that it is man's "wisdom . . . to hitch his wagon to a star," he does not hesitate, later in the same essay, to apply the same figure to the desirability of making everyday material life ideal in character. "Our aim in our writings," reads a sentence in the journals, "ought to be to make daylight shine through them."[121] And in *Spiritual Laws*,[122] we read: "The object of the man . . . is to make daylight shine through him." In one case the figure is used for a stylistic, in the other for a moral purpose. Quotations Emerson uses in similar fashion. "To the persevering mortal the blessed Immortals are swift," an aphorism from Zoroaster, is used in *Self-Reliance*[123] to show the foolishness of regret; in *Inspiration*[124] to make plain the stimulative value of steady, continuous work.

Not only may the same symbol be used in differently figurative ways, but the same idea may be typified by an indefinite number of symbols; and in this converse fashion Emerson again sees identity in variety. An interesting result of this attitude appears in his belief that religious and philosophical phrases are convertible into one another. Since all religions fundamentally rest on the same principles, the symbolic names which they employ must be interchangeable. "In matters of religion," he says, "men eagerly fasten their eyes on the differences between their creed and yours, whilst the charm of the study is in finding the agreements and identities in all the religions of men."[125] "Fortune, Minerva, Muse, Holy Ghost,— these are quaint names, too narrow to cover this unbounded substance

[118] *Representative Men: Swedenborg*, 121.
[119] *Essays* II: *The Poet*, 34.
[120] *Society and Solitude*, 28, 30.
[121] *Jour.* V, 198.
[122] *Essays* I, 161.
[123] *Essays* I, 79.
[124] *Letters, etc.*, 283.
[125] *Lectures, etc.: The Preacher*, 226–7.

. . . ineffable cause, which every fine genius has essayed to represent by some emphatic symbol, as, Thales by water, Anaximenes by air, Anaxagoras by (Νοῦς) thought, Zoroaster by fire, Jesus and the moderns by love; and the metaphor of each has become a national religion."[126] Philosophical names for the same thing are equally diverse. "Yoganidra, the goddess of illusion, Proteus, or Momus, or Gylfi's Mocking,—for the Power has many names,—is stronger than the Titans, stronger than Apollo."[127]

Other notable passages in which synonymous symbols of this kind are assembled occur in *Character*[128] with regard to superstitious fear of popular opinion; and in *Works and Days*,[129] with regard to the value of the humble moment, in other words, one important aspect of the Each and All theory itself. Illustrations from fable, religion, and science combine here to make up a frequent type of Emersonian paragraph, a collection of examples pointing at the unity of some spiritual law.

"In the Norse legend of our ancestors, Odin dwells in a fisher's hut and patches a boat. In the Hindoo legends, Hari dwells a peasant among peasants. In the Greek legend, Apollo lodges with the shepherds of Admetus, and Jove liked to rusticate among the poor Ethiopians. So, in our history, Jesus is born in a barn, and his twelve peers are fishermen. 'Tis the very principle of science that Nature shows herself best in leasts; it was the maxim of Aristotle and Lucretius; and, in modern times, of Swedenborg and of Hahnemann. The order of changes in the egg determines the age of fossil strata. So it was the rule of our poets, in the legends of fairy lore, that the fairies largest in power were the least in size."

The union of the theories of the Symbol and of Each and All has in these minor ways considerable bearing on Emerson's style. Much more important, however, is its effect on two stylistic problems which Emerson has to face as the consequence of his philosophic beliefs. Since, indeed, these two problems, more especially the second, involve consideration of all the specific qualities of diction which Emerson favored, the doctrine of Each and All has a preponderating influence on his theory and practice of style, at least so far as vocabulary is concerned.

Both problems have connection with the desirability of simplicity in language. The first is the question of the relationship of author to audience. The other and by far more important concerns the method by which Emerson found it possible, in theory anyway, to separate sharply the expression of the actual from that of the ideal, or to express them simultaneously; these, as we have seen, being the inconsistent requirements he sets the writer.

[126] *Essays* II: *Experience*, 72–3.
[127] *Conduct of Life: Illusions*, 313.
[128] *Essays* II, 98.
[129] *Society and Solitude*, 175–6.

There is much in Emerson's theories which works against consideration of the audience, at any rate against dilution or adulteration of the writer's thought to suit any incapacity there may be in the reader's intelligence. Emerson abides by his belief in Self-Reliance, which counsels him to receive with implicit trust the declarations of the Over-Soul, and to record them in their purity. But the ban against taking the reader into account does not hold in regard to the choice of vocabulary; and Emerson is often enabled, by means of his adherence to the doctrine of Each and All, to surmount the barrier to clearness raised by the other tenet. For the theory of the One and the Many makes simple phrasing, even of the ideal, possible, indeed desirable.

Since "there is no fact in nature which does not carry the whole sense of nature . . . the distinctions which we make in events and affairs, of low and high, honest and base, disappear when nature is used as a symbol." "Small and mean things," Emerson declares, "serve as well as great symbols."[130] "There is nothing small or mean to the soul. It derives as grand a joy from symbolizing the Godhead or his universe under the form of a moth or a gnat as of a Lord of Hosts."[131]

In two ways, in fact, the simple figure is superior to the great. It has, first of all, the value of a miracle: it surprises and assures of divinity. "The deepest pleasure comes . . . from the occult belief that an unknown meaning and consequence work in the common, every-day facts, and, as a panoramic or pictorial beauty can arise from it, so can a solid wisdom, when the Idea shall be seen as such which binds these gay shadows together."[132] "Must I," Emerson asks, "call the heaven and the earth a maypole and county fair with booths, or an anthill, or an old coat, in order to give you the shock of pleasure which the imagination loves and the sense of spiritual greatness? Call it a blossom, a rod, a wreath of parsley, a tamarisk-crown, a cock, a sparrow, the ear instantly hears and the spirit leaps to the trope."[133]

Another value of the simple figure is its portability. "The meaner the type by which a law is expressed, the more pungent it is, and the more lasting in the memories of men; just as we choose the smallest box or case in which any needful utensil can be carried."[134]

In these ways, the doctrine of Each and All makes simplicity in the use of symbols devoutly to be wished, and intelligibility possible. Of Emerson's attitude toward simplicity of style in general, both in theory and practice, there are many direct indications. In college days, Emerson

[130] *Essays II*: *The Poet*, 17.
[131] *Jour.* VI, 18.
[132] *Jour.* IV, 99-100.
[133] *Jour.* VI, 18-19.
[134] *Essays* II: *The Poet*, 17.

shared the admiration of his day for the floridity and inflation characteristic of contemporary oratory. His Journals contain lists of words selected for their strangeness and availability as embellishment. As a matter of fact, too, throughout his writings there are traceable occasional returns to his earlier love for grandiloquence, this being combined usually with his wish to express intensely the messages communicated to him by the Over-Soul. But for the most part this disposition to ornateness was soon replaced by recognition of the superiority of simplicity.

In 1826, at the wise maturity of 23, he wrote in his *Journals:* "The *aliquid immensum*, etc., is best left to each man's youthful and private meditations. This straining to say what is unutterable, and vain retching with the imbecile use of great words, is nauseous to sound and sense and good taste."[135] There is, moreover, much testimony to the simplicity of the sermons which Emerson delivered during his pastorate at the Second Church; and evidence that he deliberately set out to make his sermons plain in diction and allusion. At the beginning of his ministry (in 1829) he spoke to his congregation words which suggest that he had at this time found a Christian basis for the principle which he later supported by the Platonic and scientific doctrine of Each and All: "If any one hereafter should object to the want of sanctity of my style and the want of solemnity in my illustrations, I shall remind him that the language and the images of Scripture derive all their dignity from their association with divine truth, and that our Lord condescended to explain himself by allusions to every homely fact, and, if he addressed himself to the men of this age, would appeal to those arts and objects by which we are surrounded; to the printing-press and the loom, to the phenomena of steam and of gas, to free institutions and a petulant and vain nation."[136]

J. E. Cabot, Emerson's literary executor, finds, however, in the subsequent sermons (kept in manuscript at Emerson's request) few striking illustrations from everyday life[137] and there seems to be truth in his brother Charles's comment, in a letter to their Aunt Mary: "I do not doubt he may write and be a fine thinker, all alone by himself; but I think he needs to be dragged closer to people by some practical vocation."[138] This was written just before Emerson set sail for Europe in December, 1832. The desired contact was brought about by the trip, and was made stronger, after it, by residence in Concord. There, acquaintance with farmer and tradesman neighbors, his own domestic and farming duties and interests, and above all, close acquaintance with field and stream gave him fresh, individual

[135] *Memoir* I, 151-2.

[136] *Memoir* I, 149-50.

[137] *Memoir* I, 151-2.

[138] *Memoir* I, 174.

substance by which he could illustrate his philosophy in human and therefore simple terms.

Conscious of the divinity of the source of his writings, Emerson made no attempt to submit his thoughts to the level of his audience's intelligence, rather assuming their ability to rise to truth of whatever degree of elevation. But he did believe that such truth should be presented in simple and understandable language, and considered "writing down" of this kind "a main secret."[139] He had his audience of shopworkers and farmers in mind when he delivered lectures, and though he made the content of these thought of highest quality, he did his best to be simple and clear. How well he succeeded is shown by the fact that the parishioners of the church in East Lexington complained of the preacher who took Emerson's place, saying that they were simple people, but that they could understand Mr. Emerson.

Emerson did not believe in using language intelligible only to the select few. "Gauss, I believe it is," he says, "who writes books that nobody can understand but himself, and himself only in his best hours. And Peirce and Gould and others in Cambridge are piqued with the like ambition. But I fancy more the wit of Defoe, and Cervantes, and Montaigne, who make deep and abstruse things popular.'[140] "Wendell Holmes, when I offered to go to his lecture on Wordsworth, said, 'I entreat you not to go. I am forced to study effects. You and others may be able to combine popular effect with the exhibition of truths. I cannot. I am compelled to study effects.' The other day, Henry Thoreau was speaking to me about my lecture on the Anglo-American, and regretting that whatever was written for a lecture, or whatever succeeded with the audience was bad, etc. I said, I am ambitious to write something which all can read, like *Robinson Crusoe.* And when I have written a paper or a book, I see with regret that it is not solid, with a right materialistic treatment, which delights everybody."[141]

If simplicity of language can make it possible, Emerson sees advantage in bringing home eternal truth even to the dull, especially when the object is persuasion and the medium oratory. "Eloquence," he declares, "is *the power to translate a truth into language perfectly intelligible to the person*

[139] *Natural History of Intellect: Art and Criticism,* 296.

[140] *Jour.* IX, 117.

[141] The rest of the passage seems worth repeating: "Henry objected, of course, and vaunted the better lectures which only reached a few persons. Well, yesterday, he came here, and at supper Edith, understanding that he was to lecture at the Lyceum, sharply asked him, 'Whether his lecture would be a nice interesting story, such as she wanted to hear, or whether it was of those old philosophical things that she did not care about?' Henry instantly turned to her, and be thought himself, and I saw was trying to believe that he had matter that might fit Edith and Edward, who were to sit up and go to the lecture, if it was a good one for them." *Jour.* VIII, 424-5.

to whom you speak. He who would convince the worthy Mr. Dunderhead of any truth which Dunderhead does not see, must be a master of his art. Declamation is common; but such possession of thought as is here required, such practical chemistry as the conversion of a truth written in God's language into a truth in Dunderhead's language, is one of the most beautiful and cogent weapons that are forged in the shop of the Divine Artificer."[142]

Fortunately, this process of conversion is facilitated by the fact that, in any case, no matter what the mental calibre of the audience, simplicity always characterizes ideal utterance, that nearest the divine.

The connection between the divine and the simple, is shown, Emerson believes, in the language the orator uses when he is most deeply moved, when he is raised above the world of sense to the world of realities. "I belive it to be true," he says, "that when any orator at the bar or in the Senate rises in his thought, he descends in his language,—that is, when he rises to any height of thought or of passion he comes down to a language level with the ear of all his audience. It is the merit of John Brown and of Abraham Lincoln—one at Charlestown, one at Gettysburg—in the two best specimens of eloquence we have had in this country."[143] Other evidence is "the . . . charm of the ancient tragedy, and indeed of all the old literature," which is, Emerson declares, "that the persons speak simply,—speak as persons who have great good sense without knowing it, before yet the reflective habit has become the predominant habit of the mind. Our admiration of the antique is not admiration of the old, but of the natural."[144] And for Emerson nearness to the natural is nearness to the spiritual. The underlying cause of simplicity is the same in the case of either orator or writer of tragedy. Intensity in one case, naiveté in the other equally evince proximity to the divine.

So far as the audience is concerned, then, Emerson finds it possible to "speak with the vulgar, think with the wise."[145] The other and major problem which confronts him arises from his attitude toward style as it is affected by the distinction between materialism and idealism. There are occasions when he discriminates carefully between the expression of the facts of sense, and spiritual truths: the one being uttered by means of the names which common sense has given them, the other by these names used symbolically. On the other hand, he with even more frequency takes the position that the two should be expressed simultaneously; that the ideal literature should be interpretable in both ways, satisfying at the same time everyday logic and divine Reason. How are these more or less con-

[142] *Letters, etc.: Eloquence,* 130.

[143] Ibid, 125.

[144] *Essays* I: *History,* 25.

[145] *Natural History of Intellect: Art and Criticism,* 286.

tradictory requirements to be satisfied? How do they affect his choice of language?

Whether the writer divides the expression of the material from that of the ideal or unites them, it should be clear in the first place that a change to either attitude will have no great effect on his qualities of style. For even when a line is drawn setting off the language of sense from that of spirit, it is not altogether certain that the language of one will not at least suggest the other. The material, as a consequence of its unique function as expressor of the ideal, is likely to remind the reader of this capacity, even when the writer has no other purpose than to declare the common sense fact. Similarly, when the apparent fact is used to express the real, the reader—whatever may be the writer's intention—is always conscious of the ordinary meaning of the fact now used symbolically. It makes little difference whether the union of sense and spirit is slightly suggested, without the writer's connivance; or whether it is deliberately striven for—it will exist in either case. And hence the qualities of style which fit one conception will fit the other.

What now are the qualities of style capable of expressing either now the material and now the ideal, or the two in combination? On the one hand, fidelity to fact and common sense moderation—conveyed by language generally simple in character, and thus involving the use of elements drawn from every-day experience, popular speech, compression, and understatement. On the other hand, elevation and intensity—conveyed by the symbol. It must be, then, that the symbol, the ideal expression, will partake of these same characteristics which mark the expression of the actual; the ideal, too, must be communicated simply: in a style which has as its substance ordinary human event and circumstance, which is idiomatic, and which is free from the inaccuracies of excess. It should therefore be possible to justify these qualities from either point of view; to show that they are satisfactory means of conveying both the common and the transcendental.

We have seen that simplicity, obviously a fit quality of the style which aims to express the actual, is by consequence of the doctrine of Each and All readily and effectively symbolic; and that it is also close to Nature and Spirit, and hence, for this additional reason, the form of intensest expression. The same double purpose is served, likewise, by the elements which go to make up this simplicity. The language of experience is plainly the language of the hard, material fact; but it becomes, through the expansive transformation wrought by the Each and All theory, an equally desirable means of representing the ideal. The idiomatic, though earthy and of the soil and thus accurate to fact, is at the same time nearest to Nature and hence emblematic; furthermore, it is accurate on high levels because fresh, genuine, and vital. As for compression and repression, they are needful even when the language is transcendental, because the spiritual is for the most part incommunicable, words frequently only suggesting the thing; and exactness is likely to come in such a case from compulsion to use the one symbol that fits. Besides, such reticence is itself a cause of pauses that are themselves stimulating and suggestive.

It is now desirable to examine with fullness Emerson's liking for each of these elements which contribute towards a general simplicity of vocabulary, and to see the cause of his admiration in their double office.

a. Experience

Fundamental in making possible the relationship between simplicity and the symbol is the importance of experience. Experience the dualist sees as being like Nature in all respects: i.e., it is two-sided, having both physical and metaphysical value; and it is, by consequence of the canon of Each and All, emblematic, in every action which composes it, of the eternal. Hence from experience as much as from Nature the writer derives his subject-matter and his vocabulary.

The situation is not so much that experience is a teacher as that experience furnishes the material for teaching. In it the writer finds illustrations of the laws of which his intuitions have already informed him. It is his duty, having seen these material facts with their ideal significance in mind, to utilize them to show the parallelism of the actual and the spiritual. Herein is Webster praiseworthy, for he "knows what is done in the shops, and remembers and uses it in the Senate. He saw it in the shop with an eye supertabernal and supersenatorial, or it would not have steaded. He is a ship that finds the thing where it is cheap, and carries it where it is dear."[146]

Every circumstance, by consequence of the light shed on it through the belief that the One is predicable from the Many, epitomizes eternity; and hence any action, of whatever degree or kind, may serve the writer as substance. Nothing is too high or important for this purpose. "On the writer the choicest influences are concentrated,—nothing that does not go to his costly equipment: a war, an earthquake, revival of letters, the new dispensation by Jesus, or by Angels; Heaven, Hell, power, science, the *Néant*, exist to him as colors for his brush."[147] And likewise, nothing is too low or inconsequential. "Saadi and Æsop and Cervantes and Ben Jonson had . . . the tinker element and tinker experience," which Shakespeare must also have had, "as well as the courtly." Indeed, the combination, as in everything connected with writing, is, as we shall see more fully later, here also essential to genius. "A great poet must be of the middle classes."[148]

[146] *Jour.* VII, 223.

[147] *Natural History of Intellect: Art and Criticism*, 283.

[148] *Jour.* VIII, 294. See also *Jour.* VIII, 367.

Yet certain classes of experience are more significant than others. Some have an obvious material character which makes their duality of meaning all the more obvious. When the commonplace or the low or the base illustrate the ideal, when the writer follows the injunction to

> Give to barrows, trays and pans
> Grace and glimmer of romance,[149]

there is not only a magical charm in the alchemy, but the polarity which the transcendentalist loves in style is conspicuous. Accordingly when Plato, most notable example of the "balanced soul," "made transcendental distinctions, he fortified himself by drawing all his illustrations from sources disdained by orators and polite conversers; from mares and puppies; from pitchers and soup-ladles; from cooks and criers; the shops of potters, horse-doctors, butchers and fishmongers."[150]

Other experience illustrates eternal truth with peculiar success because it is universal. When the circumstance or event is common to humanity, it is both readily and attractively transferable to the field of eternal law, where it may also lead rapidly to realization of Unity. "If I," writes Emerson, "were professor of Rhetoric,—teacher of the art of writing well to young men,—I should use Dante for my text-book. Come hither, youth, and learn how the brook that flows at the bottom of your garden, or the farmer who ploughs the adjacent field, your father and mother, your debts and credits, and your web of habits are the very best basis of poetry, and the material which you must work up."[151] Emerson follows his own instruction. At the beginning of the essay on *Compensation*,[152] in telling how he came to write the discourse, he says: "The documents . . . from which the doctrine is to be drawn, charmed my fancy by their endless variety, and lay always before me, even in sleep; for they are the tools in our hands, the bread in our basket, the transactions of the street, the farm and the dwelling-house; greetings, relations, debts and credits, the influence of character, the nature and endowment of all men."

Sorrow and calamity are universal experiences which are exceptionally vital through their depth and poignancy, and may therefore, by the very law of compensation which we have just mentioned, serve the writer as capital. "The poet cannot spare any grief or pain or terror in his experience: he wants every rude stroke that has been dealt on his irritable texture." He needs fear and calamity "to construct the glossary which opens the Sanscrit of the world."[153] "In calamity, he finds new materials;

[149] *Essays* I: *Art*, 349.
[150] *Representative Men: Plato*, 55.
[151] *Jour*. VIII, 33.
[152] *Essays* I, 93.
[153] *Jour*. V, 450.

as our German poet said, 'Some god gave me the power to paint what I suffer.' He draws his rents from rage and pain. By acting rashly, he buys the power of talking wisely. Vexations and a tempest of passion only fill his sail; as the good Luther writes, 'When I am angry, I can pray well and preach well:' and, if we knew the genesis of fine strokes of eloquence, they might recall the complaisance of Sultan Amurath, who struck off some Persian heads, that his physician, Vesalius, might see the spasm in the muscles of the neck. His failures are the preparation of his victories."[154] "Was not Luther's Bible, Shakspear's Hamlet, Paul's letter, a deed as notable and far-reaching as Marengo or the dike of Arcola. Yet these were written by dint of flagging spirits. Sobs of the heart, and dull, waste, unprofitable hours, taught the master how to write to apprehensive thousands the tragedy of these same."[155]

Emerson himself knew the sweet uses of adversity and of "dull, waste, unprofitable hours." "Even in college," he tells us, "I was already content to be 'screwed' in the recitation room, if, on my return, I could accurately paint the fact in my youthful journal."[156] And later, when troubled by the fact that he was a man of the spirit rather than a man of the world and hence suffered much discomfort in society, he found literary indemnities for his mortification. He writes in his Journals in self-disdain, "A man of letters who goes into fashionable society on their terms and not on his own makes a fool of himself. Why I should be given up to that shame so many times after so much considered experience, I cannot tell. Heaven has good purposes. . . . perchance."[157] Later, he sets down one possible recompense. "The poet who is paralysed in the company of the young and beautiful, where he would so gladly shine, revenges himself by satire and taxing that with emptiness and display."[158] Such vengeance is, however, scarcely Emersonian. The result of diffidence and ill-adjustment for him is rather the serence impartiality of the essay on *Society and Solitude*. It should be mentioned, too, that there is in Emerson's writing a valuable by-product of apparent waste: the poem *Days*, in which he exculpates himself, by the very writing, from the sin of the ill-spent hours that made it possible.

Certain kinds of experience are thus widely suggestive: the ordinary, because of its salient duality; the universal human experience because of its relation to universal divine truth; and weakness and misfortune because of their keenness and depth. In this way Emerson made possible, or rather indispensable, the writer's use of common, human, and therefore simple terms; and so far, at least, the interdependence of the theories of

[154] *Representative Men: Goethe*, 263.
[155] *Jour.* IV, 445.
[156] *Jour.* IV, 437-8.
[157] *Jour.* V, 145-6.
[158] *Jour.* V, 525.

Each and All and of the Symbol, in their relation to Experience, not only enables the writer to set his thoughts down simply, but makes it highly worth while for him to do so.

If literature is to be made up of such ingredients, it is obvious that the writer must "pay his tithe"[159] as a member of society by himself working and suffering; and by mingling with those to whom life is real and earnest. The cloister, the hermitage, and the study furnish experience of far less significance than that gained in the shop, the factory, the field, the street, the home.

For action complements thought in the writer's equipment. Without it, thought "can never ripen into truth. . . . The preamble of thought, the transition through which it passes from the unconscious to the conscious, is action."[160] Without action, too, the writer's "tuition in the serene and beautiful laws,"[161] and the compositions in which he expresses these laws, will lack the vitality and reality which come only from their embodiment in personal examples. "I do not see," says Emerson, "how any man can afford, for the sake of his nerves and his nap, to spare any action in which he can partake. It is pearls and rubies to his discourse. Drudgery, calamity, exasperation, want, are instructors in eloquence and wisdom."[162]

Underlying this emphasis on experience as the stuff of writing is again the pervasive duality. Through the "mutual reaction of thought and life," through making "thought solid, and life wise," is brought about the union of sense and spirit essential to success in literature. The writer must know "the uttermost secret of toil and endurance;" and at the same time he must "never forget . . . to worship the immortal divinities who whisper to the poet and make him the utterer of melodies that pierce the ear of eternal time. . . . This twofold goodness,—the drill and the inspiration,—. . . characterizes ever the productions of great masters. The man of genius should occupy the whole space between God or pure mind and the multitude of uneducated men. He must draw from the infinite Reason, on one side; and he must penetrate into the heart and sense of the crowd, on the other. From one, he must draw his strength; to the other, he must owe his aim. The one yokes him to the real; the other, to the apparent. At one pole is Reason; at the other, Common Sense. If he be defective at either extreme of the scale, his philosophy will seem low and utilitarian, or it will appear too vague and indefinite for the uses of life."[163]

[159] *Nature, etc.: Literary Ethics*, 182.
[160] *Nature, etc.: The American Scholar*, 94–5.
[161] *Nature, etc.: Literary Ethics*, 178.
[162] *Nature, etc.: The American Scholar*, 95.
[163] *Nature, etc.: Literary Ethics*, 181–2.

Substance and reinforcement are not all that the writer derives from the daily details of experience. From them comes also his vocabulary. "My garden is my dictionary,"[164] Emerson writes, and means it literally. He finds interest in the reciprocal influence of life on language and language on life. During the Civil War he comments in his Journal: "I am always struck with the speed with which every new interest, party, or way of thinking gets its *bon-mot* and name and so adds a new word to language. Thus Higginson, and Livermore, Hosmer, and the fighting chaplains give necessity and vogue to 'muscular Christianity.' The language of the day readily suggested to some wit to call hell 'a military necessity.' "[165] This interplay of words and deed makes plain that "If it were only for a vocabulary, the scholar would be covetous of action. Life is our dictionary. Years are well spent in country labors; in town; in the insight into trades and manufactures; in frank intercourse with many men and women; in science; in art; to the one end of mastering in all their facts a language by which to illustrate and embody our perceptions. I learn immediately from any speaker how much he has already lived, through the poverty or the splendor of his speech. Life lies behind us as the quarry from whence we get tiles and copestones for the masonry of to-day. This is the way to learn grammar. Colleges and books only copy the language which the field and the work-yard made."[166]

It is needless to point out that a vocabulary so vital will be simple and understandable. But the connection between experience and simplicity in language and illustration does not end here. It is strengthened by the interrelationship between the Each and All theory, Self-Reliance, and Emerson's methods of writing. In the first place, the Each and All theory assures the writer that the most common thoughts, objects, and actions are miniature expressions of Spirit. In the second place, Self-Reliance directs that the individual should trust and utilize what the Over-Soul indicates to him is peculiarly his to think, to remember, and to say. In the third place, the two canons cooperate to effect the conviction that personal, individual, original experience, thoughts, memories, and symbols conceal, though under the most unpromising exterior, a far-reaching significance that makes them treasurable and worthy of expression. And in the fourth place, here is the justification of Emerson's practice of setting down in his journals the golden thought, experience, or symbol of the moment. For he did so in the assurance that the infinite relationship of every particle would some day make clear the right literary use of all these divinely inspired fragments.

[164] *Jour.* IV, 234.

[165] *Jour.* X, 14.

[166] *Nature, etc.: The American Scholar*, 97–8.

In the detailed consideration that follows, it will be seen that the theories of Self-Reliance and Each and All meet and sometimes indistinguishably merge. To see their relationship to one another as it affects the use of personal materials, it is perhaps best to begin by remembering that Self-Reliance is not egotism. It does not encourage freakish, cranky writing, or the literature which rejoices in wilful isolation of opinion. It is rather based on the confidence that the divine voice may be heard more or less distinctly by every man, and that, as a result, every man is a sharer in inspiration and in the knowledge of universal truths. With this is joined, so far as our present subject is concerned, the fact that there are many experiences which are common to humanity. If therefore any man's experience seems to him significant of universal truths, self-reliance gives him reason to believe that the account of his actions so looked at will suit everybody's case and hence be interesting to all. When Emerson writes: "What pleases me will please many,"[167] he means nothing more offensively personal than: What pleases the universal man in me will please the universal man in others. Thus in regard to writing, self-reliance, by certifying our universality, enables us to "discover how rich we are. Our history, we are sure, is quite tame: we have nothing to write, nothing to infer. But our wiser years still run back to the despised recollections of childhood, and always we are fishing up some wonderful article out of that pond; until by and by we begin to suspect that the biography of the one foolish person we know is, in reality, nothing less than the miniature paraphrase of the hundred volumes of the Universal History."[168]

A most interesting passage from the *Journals* will not only serve to make clear the application of this principle to literature, but will illustrate Emerson's practical use of it in his own writing. "I please myself with getting my nail-box set in the snuggest corner of the barn-chamber and well filled with nails, and gimlet, pincers, screw-driver and chisel. Herein I find an old joy of youth, of childhood, which perhaps all domestic children share,—the catlike love of garrets, barns and corn-chambers, and of the conveniences of long housekeeping. It is quite genuine. When it occurs to-day, I ask, Have others the same? Once I should not have thought of such a question. What I loved, I supposed all children loved and knew, and therefore I did not name them. We were at accord. But much conversation, much comparison, apprises us of difference. The first effect of this new learning is to incline us to hide our tastes. As they differ, we must be wrong. Afterwards some person comes and wins *éclat* by simply describing this old but concealed fancy of ours. Then we immediately learn to value all the parts of our nature, to rely on them as self-authorized and that to publish them is to please others. So now the

[167] *Jour.* IV, 212.
[168] *Essays* I: *Intellect*, 334.

nail-box figures for its value in my Journal."[169] And one likes to note that the sentences in the above regarding the nail-box and the "catlike love of garrets" eventually find their proper place in the essay on *Prudence*.[170]

Self-Reliance, then, asserts that the individual's liking, through his share in universality, is everybody's liking. This dictum easily and imperceptibly aligns itself with the theory of Each and All. For the attractiveness of the record of anybody's experience proceeds not only from the fact that it is everybody's experience, but from the fact that it is seen in the light of general law; that a strong classifying thought has been exerted upon it and has made use of it for illustration or symbol.

The psychological process is this: "The new deed is yet a part of life,—remains for a time immersed in our unconscious life. In some contemplative hour it detaches itself from the life like a ripe fruit, to become a thought of the mind. Instantly it is raised, transfigured; the corruptible has put on incorruption. Henceforth it is an object of beauty, however base its origin and neighborhood."[171]

And when it is expressed in literature, the enhanced value remains. "Each truth that a writer acquires is a lantern which he turns full on what facts and thoughts lay already in his mind, and behold, all the mats and rubbish which had littered his garret become precious. Every trivial fact in his private biography becomes an illustration of this new principle, revisits the day, and delights all men by its piquancy and new charm."[171] Thus "Goethe's account of the feelings of a bridegroom. The subjective is made objective. That which we had *only lived*, and not thought and not valued, is now seen to have the greatest beauty as picture; and as we value a Dutch painting of a kitchen, or a frolic of blackguards, or a beggar catching a flea, when the scene itself we should avoid, so we see worth in things we had slighted these many years. A making it a subject of *thought*, the glance of the Intellect raises it."[173]

Though the ordinary man cherishes the facts of his individual experience, he thinks them trivial and unworthy of record. He has but vaguely and unconsciously apprehended the general law to which they relate. When the great writer records such facts, "Men say, Where did he get this? and think there was something divine in his life. But no; they have myriads of facts just as good, would they only get a lamp to ransack their attics withal." Yet "we are all wise. The difference between persons is not in wisdom but in art. I knew, in an academical club, a person who always deferred to me; who, seeing my whim for writing, fancied that my

[169] *Jour.* IV, 283-4.
[170] *Essays* I, 227.
[171] *Nature, etc.: The American Scholar*, 96.
[172] *Essays* I: *Intellect*, 332.
[173] *Jour.* IV, 99.

experiences had somewhat superior; whilst I saw that his experiences were as good as mine. Give them to me and I would make the same use of them. He held the old; he holds the new; I had the habit of tacking together the old and the new which he did not use to exercise. This may hold in the great examples. Perhaps, if we should meet Shakspeare we should not be conscious of any steep inferiority; no, but of a great equality,—only that he possessed a strange skill of using, of classifying his facts, which we lacked."[174]

It now becomes evident not only that the genius is characterized (as we saw in the chapter on the Symbol) by his power of metonymy and by the accompanying perception of identity in variety, but that he has extraordinary ability to see universality in the facts of his private experience. It is apparent, too, that he has confidence, which the usual writer lacks, to use this ability. "Dante's praise," Emerson says, "is that he dared to write his autobiography in colossal cipher, or into universality."[175] The genius has Self-Reliance. Again this doctrine meets and coalesces with that of Each and All.

This particular gift of genius Emerson calls "detachment by illumination."[176] He exclaims: "How much self-reliance it implies to write a true description of anything, for example, Wordsworth's picture of skating; that leaning back on your heels and stopping in mid-career. So simple a fact no common man would have trusted himself to detach as a thought."[177]

Self-Reliance alone makes originality possible, and originality is an inevitable constituent of genius. Originality, of course, implies newness; and "Novelty in the means by which we arrive at the old universal ends is the test of the presence of the highest power."[178] The connection between genius and the utilization of one's own experience as substance for writing now becomes plain. For nothing is so likely to be productive of novelty as the value a man attaches to the facts of his private experience. Hence confidence in the literary value of such actions, and in the individual impressions made by those actions, is a mark of genius.

The necessary corrective of the whim and conceit to which this conception might give rise is supplied in the fact that by Self-Reliance Emerson means "reliance on God,"[179] not egotism. Self-Reliance is a faith that whatever the Spirit indicates to the individual as important, is such because of the divine source of the intimation. If, then, the intuitions

[174] *Essays* I: *Intellect*, 332–3.

[175] *Essays* II: *The Poet*, 37.

[176] *Jour.* IX, 309.

[177] *Jour.* IV, 398.

[178] *Natural History of Intellect: Instinct and Inspiration*, 71.

[179] *Miscellanies: The Fugitive Slave Law—Lecture at New York*, 236.

find good in the facts of the writer's experience, so does he perforce. Originality, therefore, is an obedience to the dictates of the soul; and if the soul haloes some events in one's life, those become thereby worthy of literary use.

That caprice and vainglory play no part in Self-Reliance as it regards the literary conversion of the personal is evident in the perfect naturalness of the process by which certain events and memories acquire their strange spiritual significance. "Observe . . . the impossibility of antedating this act," Emerson directs us. "In its grub state" the deed "cannot fly, it cannot shine, it is a dull grub. But suddenly, without observation, the selfsame thing unfurls beautiful wings, and is an angel of wisdom."[180] "My will," says Emerson, "never gave the images in my mind the rank they now take. The regular course of studies, the years of academical and professional education have not yielded me better facts than some idle books under the bench at the Latin School."[181]

Originality, therefore, grows out of the natural, unanalyzed intimations of Spirit. In the writer's peculiar behalf, these intimations invest certain parts of his own experience with a universal significance. Trusting in their sacredness, he has self-reliance to find here the matter of his writing. He looks at the same time into his heart and into his experience, and writes. "Those facts, words, persons, which dwell in" the writer's "memory without his being able to say why, remain because they have a relation to him not less real for being as yet unapprehended. They are symbols of value to him as they can interpret parts of his consciousness which he would vainly seek words for in the conventional images of books and other minds. What attracts my attention shall have it, as I will go to the man who knocks at my door, whilst a thousand persons as worthy go by it, to whom I give no regard. It is enough that these particulars speak to me. A few anecdotes, a few traits of character, manners, face, a few incidents, have an emphasis in your memory out of all proportion to their apparent significance if you measure them by the ordinary standards. They relate to your gift. Let them have their weight, and do not reject them and cast about for illustration and facts more usual in literature. What your heart thinks great, is great. The soul's emphasis is always right."[182]

Thus an unseen hand touches particular memories with a special significance. But God helps those who help themselves, and nothing forbids the writer to stretch out his own hand to meet the unseen. Without perceiving his eventual use of a fact, he is assured by self-reliance that any part of his experience may become important, and so he records

[180] *Nature, etc.: The American Scholar*, 96.
[181] *Essays* I: *Spiritual Laws*, 133.
[182] *Essays* I: *Spiritual Laws*, 144–5.

it if only because it is his. And even if this fact is not of the elect, he cannot go wrong in expressing it. For here he has to support him the coöperation of the Each and All theory, assuring him of the symbolic character of every fact however small.

Therefore when the writer "sees some figure for a moment in an expressive attitude and surroundings . . . . without hesitating because it is a mere purposeless fragment, he paints out that figure with what skill and energy he has."[183] Emerson tells us, too, that this holds of his own practice. "Each new fact I look upon, as this steaming of hot air from the wide fields upward, is a new word that I learn and have, well assured the use for it will come presently, as the boy learns with good hope his Latin vocabulary."[184] "I am a matchmaker," he declares in another passage, "and delight in nothing more than in finding the husband or mate of the trivial fact I have long carried in my memory (unable to offer any reason for the emphasis I gave it), until now, suddenly, it shows itself as the true symbol or expression of some abstraction."[185] He tells us concerning his voyage to England: "Sometimes a memorable fact turns up, which you have long had a vacant niche for, and seize with the joy of a collector."[186] And he finds in old age the solace that "the lonely thought, which seemed so wise, yet half-wise, half-thought, because it cast no light abroad, is suddenly matched in our mind by its twin, by its sequence, or next related analogy, which gives it instantly radiating power, and justifies the superstitious instinct with which we have hoarded it."[187]

It now becomes clear how Emerson's method of keeping a journal accords with his doctrines of Each and All and Self-Reliance. He believes that the attractiveness of personal experience when made a subject of thought, when shown in its universal relations, "admonishes us instantly if that hour and object can be so valuable, why not every hour and event in our life, if passed through the same process?"[188] Acting in concurrence with this conviction, he gathers in his journals anecdotes, proverbs, data of various kinds, and makes entries of the passing thought, emotion, or symbol—all in the confidence that they may some day find their proper place and relation. So he takes full advantage of the infinite possibility of expansion which exists in every moment's experience. So, too, he need not rest content with pressing favorite blossoms in his memory, but may cull them in their first bloom and keep them fresh against the day when they are to be entwined in a garland of such flowers.

[183] *Jour.* IX, 309.
[184] *Jour.* V, 418-9.
[185] *Jour.* IX, 272-3.
[186] *English Traits: Voyage to England*, 32.
[187] *Society and Solitude: Old Age*, 330.
[188] *Jour.* IV, 100.

That this interaction of the dicta of Self-Reliance and Each and All is a force which works for simplicity in style is easily seen. For it is trivialities, the joys and sorrows of childhood and youth, the "most seemingly inadequate and mean occasions"[189] which illustrate to the individual his theories of life and his visions of beauty: "the fear of boys, and dogs, and ferules, the love of little maids and berries,"[190] "hearing an unwashed boy spell or cipher in his class, or seeing the blush upon the cheek of a school-girl, or watching the transmission of the candlelight through his closed fingers, or listening long to the sound made by tinkling a glass tumbler or touching the key of a piano."[191]

Another cause contributing to simplicity in diction is the indifferency of the subject. Just as any kind of experience may furnish examples and symbols for the details of writing, so the whole composition may be written on any topic. Again the theory of Each and All is responsible. It makes every subject pertinent. Enabling utilization of the small, the common, the domestic, the commercial, the near in time and place, it is a great influence tending to simplicity in style.

Size has nothing to do with the availabilty of a subject. "I say to Lidian that in composition the *What* is of no importance compared with the *How*. The most tedious of all discourses are on the subject of the Supreme Being."[192] "The elasticity of the present object . . . makes all the agnitudes and magnates quite unnecessary. This is what we mean when we say your subject is absolutely indifferent. You need not write the History of the World, nor the Fall of Man, nor King Arthur, nor Iliad, nor Christianity; but write of hay, or of cattle shows, or trade sales, or of a ship, or of Ellen, or Alcott, or of a couple of schoolboys, if only you can be the fanatic of your subject, and find a fibre reaching from it to the core of your heart, so that all your affection and all your thought can freely play."[193]

The everyday domestic and business affairs are as good topics as any. The artist, Emerson says, "is very well convinced that the great moments of life are those in which his own house, his own body, the tritest and nearest ways and words and things have been illuminated into prophets and teachers. What else is it to be a poet? What are his garland and singing-robes? What but a sensibility so keen that the scent of an elder-blow, or the timber-yard and corporation-works of a nest of pismires is event enough for him,—all emblems and personal appeals to him. . . . There is no subject that does not belong to him,—politics, economy, manufactures and stock-brokerage, as much as sunsets and souls; only,

[189] *Jour.* III, 228.
[190] *Nature, etc.: The American Scholar*, 97.
[191] *Jour.* III, 228-9.
[192] *Jour.* IV, 211.
[193] *Jour.* IX, 207.

these things, placed in their true order, are poetry; displaced, or put in kitchen order, they are unpoetic."[194] "Herrick's merit lies in his power of glorifying common and base objects in his perfect verse. He pushes this privilege of the poet very far, in the wantonness of his power. He delights to show the Muse not nice or squeamish, but treading with firm and elastic step in sordid places, taking no more pollution than the sunbeam, which shines alike on the carrion and the violet."[195] "He found his subject where he stood, between his feet, in his house, pantry, barn, poultry-yard, in his village, neighbors' gossip and scandal."[196]

Hence travel is unnecessary for the writer. Emerson concedes that the authors "who have written out their vein" are "moved by a commendable prudence" when they "sail for Greece or Palestine, follow the trapper into the prairie, or ramble round Algiers, to replenish their merchantable stock."[197] But in general he considers travelling "Boswellism." "Illustrate, eternize your own woodhouse," he urges. "It is much cheaper, and quite possible to any resolute thinker."[198] "Given the insight" the writer "will find as many beauties and heroes and strokes of genius close by him as Dante or Shakspeare beheld. It was in a cold moor farm, in a dingy country inn, that Burns found his fancy so sprightly."[199] " 'Donde hai tu pigliato tante coglionerie?' and where did you pick up all this heap of fripperies, Messer Lodovico Ariosto? said the duke to the poet. 'Here in your court, your Highness,' he replied."[200]

As remoteness in place is unnecessary and in general undesirable in a subject, so is remoteness in time. Emerson advises against writing "modern antiques like Landor's *Pericles*, or Goethe's *Iphigenia*. . . . They are paste jewels." They are likely to be unnatural and to that extent insincere. He does admit that "You may well take an ancient subject where the form is incidental merely, like Shakspeare's plays, and the treatment and dialogue is simple, and most modern."[201] "I know," he grants, "there is entertainment and room for talent in the artist's selection of ancient or remote subjects; as when the poet goes to India, or to Rome, or to Persia, for his fable."[202] But he gives higher praise to Goethe, who, by virtue of his "power to unite the detached atoms again by their own law, . . . has clothed our modern existence with poetry. Amid littleness and detail, he detected the Genius of life, the old cunning

[194] *Letters, etc.: Poetry and Imagination, Veracity*, 37.
[195] *Memoir* II, 721.
[196] *Natural History of Intellect: Art and Criticism*, 296.
[197] *Nature, etc.: The American Scholar*, 97.
[198] *Jour.* III, 340.
[199] *Miscellanies*, 632.
[200] *Jour.* VI, 110.
[201] *Jour.* VI, 400.
[202] *Letters, etc.: Poetry and Imagination, Veracity*, 36.

Proteus, nestling close beside us, and showed that the dulness and prose we ascribe to the age was only another of his masks:—

> His very flight is presence in disguise:

—that he had put off a gay uniform for a fatigue dress, and was not a whit less vivacious or rich in Liverpool or the Hague than once in Rome or Antioch."[203] Even "the poor Pickwick stuff," as Emerson calls it, "teaches this, that prose and parlors and shops and city windows, the tradesman's dinner, and such matters, are as good materials in a skilful hand for interest and art as palaces and revolutions."[204] And Carlyle is commendable for a like reason, having given, in his books, "the first domestication of the modern system, with its infinity of details, into style."[205]

If, then, "the test or measure of poetic genius is the power to read the poetry of affairs,—to fuse the circumstance of to-day," if nearness in time and place is to be sought, it is obvious that the American writer should choose the contemporary American subject, should "convert the vivid energies acting at this hour in New York and Chicago and San Francisco, into universal symbols."[206] "Of all absurdities," Emerson exclaims, "this of some foreigner proposing to take away my rhetoric and substitute his own, and amuse me with pelican and stork, instead of thrush and robin; palm-trees and shittim-wood, instead of sassafras and hickory,—seems the most needless."[207] Emerson had great faith in this country as a literary field, but did not believe it had been worked deeply. He urged this on Carlyle as a reason for taking up residence here. "Here are rich materials for the philosopher and poet, and, what is more to your purpose as an artist . . . we have had in these parts no one philosopher or poet to put a sickle to the prairie wheat."[208] And in *The Poet* he says: "We have yet had no genius in America, with tyrannous eye, which knew the value of our incomparable materials, and saw, in the barbarism and materialism of the times, another carnival of the same gods he so much admires in Homer; then in the Middle Age; then in Calvinism. Banks and tariffs, the newspaper and caucus, Methodism and Unitarianism, are flat and dull to dull people, but rest on the same foundations of wonder as the town of Troy and the temple at Delphi, and are as swiftly passing away. Our log-rolling, our stumps and their politics, our fisheries, our Negroes and Indians, our boats . . . , the northern trade, the southern planting, the western clear-

[203] *Representative Men: Goethe*, 273–4.

[204] *English Traits*, 383-4.

[205] *Natural History of Intellect: Papers from the Dial, Past and Present*, 390.

[206] *Letters, etc.: Poetry and Imagination, Veracity*, 34.

[207] *Representative Men: Swedenborg*, 136.

[208] *C. E. Corr.* I, 120.

ing, Oregon and Texas, are yet unsung. Yet America is a poem in our eyes; its ample geography dazzles the imagination, and it will not wait long for metres."[209]

To the writer nothing human is alien. Good to report are whatsoever things that are homely and near at hand, whatsoever things that are personal, whatsoever things that are common to mankind. In other words, we may almost say: whatsoever things that are expressible simply. But the stress laid on the importance of daily bread as the writer's food should not cause forgetfulness of the transubstantiation brought about by his holy use of it. It provides a means of communing with the divine. Everyday experience derives its availability from its symbolic, its ideal value. If the commonplace has not been enhanced by a change to something rich and strange, if it has not been beautified by the magic wrought by the universal law which has power over it, it lacks its chief charm and merit.

Moreover, it is unsatisfactory from the artistic as well as the transcendental point of view. The result of failure to see the private experience in a universal light Emerson thus describes: "Every one would be poet if his intellectual digestion were perfect; if the grass and carrots passed through all the four stomachs, and became pure milk. But in Crumplehorn's cream, there is sometimes a tang of turnip; and in the gay pictures of the orator, a reminder now and then of autobiography,—staring eyes of duns, or schoolmasters, or cousins, or critics, who have tormented him, far on this side of heaven."[210]

The exceptional power of convertibility into ideal expression which ordinary events and circumstances possess has two important effects: it makes humanity an inestimable constituent of the writer's character; and it accords with the democratization of literature.

The writer who gathers his material and chooses his topics from the everyday life around him must have in himself and in his writing the quality of humanity: the ability to sympathize with and interpret the actions, thoughts, and feelings of the members of all classes of society. Scott, for example, "by nature, by his reading and taste an aristocrat, in a time and country which easily gave him that bias . . . had the virtues and graces of that class," but "not less his eminent humanity delighted in the sense and virtue and wit of the common people. In his own household and neighbors he found characters and pets of humble class, with whom he established the best relation,—small farmers and tradesmen, shepherds, fishermen, gypsies, peasant-girls, crones,—and came with these into real ties of mutual help and goodwill. From these originals he

[209] *Essays* II: *The Poet*, 37–8.
[210] *Jour.* IX, 546.

drew so genially his Jeanie Deans, his Dinmonts and Edie Ochiltrees, Caleb Balderstones and Fairservices, Cuddie Headriggs, Dominies, Meg Merrilies, and Jenny Rintherouts, full of life and reality; making these, too, the pivots on which the plots of his stories turn; and meantime without one word of brag of this discernment,—nay, this extreme sympathy reaching down to every beggar and beggar's dog, and horse and cow."[211] Plutarch has the same quality. "Nothing touches man but he feels to be his. . . . A man of society, of affairs; upright, practical; a good son, husband, father and friend,—he has a taste for common life, and knows the court, the camp and the judgment-hall, but also the forge, farm, kitchen and cellar, and every utensil and use."[212]

For the conversion of every kind of human element into writing, duality of vision is necessary, as always. The writer "must have a sensuous eye, but an intellectual co-perception."[213] He must go behind the coat to the character of the man, and find there universality. He must regard every human action as significant of the spirit which animated it. In mankind, as in Nature, he must view outer semblances as symbolic of inner realities.

Emerson found the preaching of his day deficient in both respects. "I wish," he says, "to find in my preacher that power to illuminate and warm and purify . . . and . . . that power to clothe every secret and abstract thought in its corresponding material symbol."[214] But his wishes were not gratified. Not only did the Calvinist and even the Unitarian hold by outworn formulas, by traditions and dogmas rather than truth, but they illustrated them either not at all or by second-hand reference to Biblical stories and parables. In his Journals Emerson frequently gives vent to his dissatisfaction and irritation at going to church and having experiences like that described in the Divinity College *Address*:[215] "A snow-storm was falling around us. The snow-storm was real, the preacher merely spectral, and the eye felt the sad contrast in looking at him, and then out of the window behind him into the beautiful meteor of the snow. He had lived in vain. He had no one word intimating that he had laughed or wept, was married or in love, had been commended, or cheated, or chagrined. . . . Not one fact in all his experience had he yet imported into his doctrine." Bitterly Emerson declares: "The clergy are the etiquette or Chinese Empire of our American Society. They are here that we may not be fed and bedded and die and be buried as dogs, but, in the want of dignity, we may be treated to a sufficiency of parade

[211] *Miscellanies: Walter Scott*, 465–6.

[212] *Lectures, etc.: Plutarch*, 299.

[213] Ibid, 298–9.

[214] *Jour.* X, 214.

[215] *Nature, etc.*, 137–8.

and gentle gradations of salutation at coming and parting. If anybody dies and grieves us to the heart, so that the people might be melted to tears by a hearty word, the minister shuts his lips and preaches on the miracles, or the parables, or Solomon's Temple, because the family have not *had up their note;* if any new outrage on law or any pregnant event fills the mind of people with queries and omens, the pulpit is dumb."[216]

The preacher cannot deliver successful sermons unless he considers the individuals in his audience; unless his humanity is broad enough to make him see the necessity of suiting his material to their needs. When Emerson was a young divinity student, he gave himself this advice: "Take care, take care that your sermon is not a recitation; that it is a sermon to Mr. A. and Mr. B. and Mr. C."[217] In this regard, Emerson found much to admire in the preaching of Edward Taylor, the Methodist minister whose fame spread far from the sailors' mission he conducted in Boston. "How can he," Emerson exclaims, "transform all those whiskered, shaggy, untrim tarpaulins into sons of light and hope, by seeing the man within the sailor, seeing them to be sons, lovers, brothers, husbands."[218]

If the preacher, then, remembers that he is speaking to human beings, that his office is to reform and relieve, he will avoid empty generalities. "At church today," Emerson records, "I felt how unequal is this match of words against things. Cease, O thou unauthorized talker, to prate of consolation, and resignation, and spiritual joys, in neat and balanced sentences. For I know these men who sit below. . . . There is Mr. T—, the shoemaker, whose daughter has gone mad, and he is looking up through his spectacles to hear what you can offer for his case. Here is my friend, whose scholars are all leaving him, and he knows not what to turn his hand to, next. Here is my wife, who has come to church in hope of being soothed and strengthened after being wounded by the sharp tongue of a slut in her house. Here is the stage-driver who has the jaundice, and cannot get well. Here is B., who failed last week, and he is looking up. O speak things, then, or hold thy tongue."[219]

When the preacher does speak "things," the hearer, even if his own particular case is not touched on, yet recognizes the universality of the teaching. "Everything is my cousin, and when he speaks things, I immediately feel he is touching some of my relations, and I am uneasy, but whilst he deals in words I can slumber and sleep."[220]

[216] *Jour.* VI, 423-4.

[217] *Society and Solitude,* 371-2.

[218] *Jour.* IV, 156.

[219] *Jour.* V, 200-1.

[220] *Jour.* IV, 277.

From what source is the preacher to receive the insight and the material which will give his sermons human comprehension and sympathy? From his own life. The lesson should be impressed on a young man just entering the ministry "that a people can well afford to settle large incomes on a man, that he may marry, buy and sell, and administer his own good, if the practical lesson that he thus learns he can translate into general terms and yield them its poetry from week to week."[221] Concerning his great-grandfather, Rev. Joseph Emerson, Emerson tells us that in his "old diary . . . ending in the year 1736, one easily sees the useful egotism of our old Puritan clergy. The minister *experienced* life for his flock. He gave prominence to all his economy and history for the benefit of the parish. His cow and horse and pig did duty next Sunday in the pulpit. All his haps are providences. If he keeps school, marries, begets children, if his house burns, if his children have the measles, if he is thrown from his horse, if he buys a negro, and Dinah misbehaves, if he buys or sells his chaise—all his adventures are fumigated with prayer and praise—he improves next Sunday the new circumstance,—and the willing flock are contented with this consecretion of one man's adventures for the benefit of them all, inasmuch as that one is on the right level and therefore a fair representative."[222]

In the prayers and sermons of another relative, the Rev. Ezra Ripley, Emerson found a like merit. Even though he saw that Dr. Ripley idealized nothing and was hidebound by tradition,[223] Emerson recognized also that his contact with the practicalities of life gave his words a loving-kindness impossible to the utterances of the more learned and equally dogmatic city clergy, "the Boston preachers of proprieties—the fair house of Seem."[224] Such country preachers, through "their inevitable acquaintance with the outer nature of man, and with his strict dependence on sun and rain and wind and frost,—wood, worm, cow and bird, get an education to the Homeric simplicity"[225] which makes their words affectingly human. The result of such preaching, too, depends on the humanity of its hearers. "Sunday," notes Emerson, "I could not help remarking . . . how much humanity was in the preaching of my good uncle. . . . The rough farmers had their hands at their eyes repeatedly. But the old hardened sinners, the arid, educated men, ministers and others, were dry as stones."[226] The "good uncle," Dr. Ripley's son, Samuel, was also an example of the "true preacher," who, Emerson says, "can be known by this,

[221] *Jour.* IV, 232-3.
[222] *Jour.* VII, 338-9.
[223] *Jour.* IV, 234.
[224] *Jour.* III, 556.
[225] *Jour.* III, 556.
[226] *Jour.* IV, 379.

that he deals out to the people his life,—life passed through the fire of thought."[227]

Humanity (with an accompanying "Homeric simplicity") is necessary to the preacher—to every user of words, for "the capital secret of his profession" is to see "the symbolical character of life"[228] and "to convert life into truth."[229] This correspondence between literature and life makes the democratization of literature inevitable. When the people control the politics, they also control the books. Democracy has brought a new audience, and with it new topics. "The decline of the privileged orders, all over the world; the advance of the Third Estate; the transformation of the laborer into reader and writer has compelled the learned and the thinkers to address them. Chiefly in this country, the common school has added two or three audiences: once, we had only the boxes; now, the galleries and the pit."[230]

With these additions has come a change in subject-matter. Few now are so poor as to do reverence to the name of king. Royalty has lost its glamour, wealth its beauty. "What is good that is said or written now lies nearer to men's business and bosoms than of old. What is good goes now to all. . . . Prester John no more shall be heard of. Tamerlane and the Buccaneers vanish before Texas, Oregon territory, the Reform Bill, the abolition of slavery and of capital punishment, questions of education, and the Reading of Reviews; and in these all men take part. The human race have got possession, and it is all questions that pertain to their interest, outward or inward, that are now discussed, and many words leap out alive from bar-rooms, Lyceums, Committee Rooms, that escape out of doors and fill the world with their thunder."[231]

Now is there room for a poet like Burns, "the poet," Emerson calls him, "of the poor, anxious, cheerful, working humanity," "of gray hodden and the guernsey coat and the blouse. He has given voice to all the experiences of common life; he has endeared the farm house and cottage, patches and poverty, beans and barley; ale, the poor man's wine; hardship; the fear of debt; the dear society of weans and wife, of brothers and sisters, proud of each other, knowing so few and finding amends for want and obscurity in books and thoughts. What a love of Nature, and, shall I say it? of middle-class nature. Not like Goethe, in the stars, or like Byron, in the ocean, or Moore, in the luxurious East, but in the homely landscape which the poor see around them,—bleak leagues of pasture and stubble,

[227] *Nature, etc.: Address*, 138.

[228] *Jour.* IV, 232.

[229] *Nature, etc.: Address*, 138.

[230] *Natural History of Intellect: Art and Criticism*, 283–4.

[231] *Jour.* IV, 94-5.

ice and sleet and rain and snow-choked brooks; birds, hares, field-mice, thistles and heather, which he daily knew."[232]

"God said, I am tired of kings,"

rings out Emerson's *Boston Hymn*, in defiance to the oppressors of the poor and the slave-owners in particular. Emerson's individualism makes him an ardent democrat. He sees in each man divine possibilities, and in popular institutions spiritual significance. The "fishers and choppers and ploughmen" who constitute the American state are fit emblems for its literature. Thus the New Hampshire or Vermont boy who "*teams it, farms it, peddles*"[233] is Emerson's model of self-reliance. He finds illustrations of the law of Prudence equally in the maxims of State Street and the haymaker.[234] Our Congress and other public assemblies serve as tests of character.[235] The friendliness of American laws and customs towards women's rights is a sign of chivalry.[236] He finds an instance of the right kind of power in the "rough-riders,—legislators in shirt-sleeves, Hoosier, Sucker, Wolverine, Badger," for "the instinct of the people is right."[237]

To have and to hold experience: this is the desire of the writer who wishes a style which is an amalgam of gold and the baser metals. This experience is not to be of an out-of-the-way character gained in out-of-the-way places. Divinity and universality dwell everywhere, but most significantly here and now in the most familiar surroundings. Hence the ideal style is the simple style; the simple language which is descriptive of simple things is that in which the material and the ideal best come together. The writer, accordingly, sees, cherishes, and shows the beauty and the poetry in the ordinary events of his own life and his neighbor's. This entails a community of thought and feeling and action which stirs into his writings that universal nutriment, the milk of human kindness. This same unanimity, furthermore, brings his writings into line with the worldwide movement toward democracy in literature and life.

The duality of the simple experience and its connection with the Symbol and the Each and All theory, together with some reference to the desirability of humanity and democracy as elements in literature, appear eloquently in a paragraph from *The American Scholar*,[238] which will serve to collect and summarize these points: "The literature of the poor, the feelings of the child, the philosophy of the street, the meaning of house-

[232] *Miscellanies: Robert Burns*, 441–2.
[233] *Essays* I: *Self-Reliance*, 76.
[234] *Essays* I: *Prudence*, 234–5.
[235] *Essays* II: *Character*, 91–2.
[236] *Essays* II: *Manners*, 150.
[237] *Conduct of Life: Power*, 63.
[238] *Nature, etc.*, 111.

hold life, are the topics of the time. It is a great stride. It is a sign—is it not?—of new vigor when the extremities are made active, when currents of warm life run into the hands and the feet. I ask not for the great, the remote, the romantic; what is doing in Italy or Arabia; what is Greek art, or Provençal minstrelsy; I embrace the common, I explore and sit at the feet of the familiar, the low. Give me insight into to-day, and you may have the antique and future worlds. What would we really know the meaning of? The meal in the firkin; the milk in the pan; the ballad in the street; the news of the boat; the glance of the eye; the form and the gait of the body;—show me the ultimate reason of these matters; show me the sublime presence of the highest spiritual cause lurking, as always it does lurk, in these suburbs and extremities of nature; let me see every trifle bristling with the polarity that ranges it instantly on an eternal law; and the shop, the plough, and the ledger referred to the like cause by which light undulates and poets sing."

b. Idiom

The eternal singer of the everyday must have exceptional command of his middle register. For that most of his songs are written; and it is because of his assurance there that he succeeds with those that do require passing from chest-tones to head-tones. The writer who usually mingles in his sentences the actual and the ideal, and only occasionally emphasizes their differences, must write with certainty the medial style in which the two are joined if he is to diverge from it to one or the other extremity. He must be able, like Shakspeare, to maintain the "level tone which is the tone of high and low alike, and most widely understood."[239] The keynote of such a style is of course simplicity. The writer must have "the perfect, plain style" with which Emerson credits Herrick, "from which he can soar to a fine, lyric delicacy, or descend to coarsest sarcasm, without losing his firm footing."[240]

Equivalent to a "perfect, plain style" is for Emerson "a noble idiomatic English."[240] His liking for the idiomatic is not to be dissociated from his fondness for simple expression. To idiom, indeed, he attributes the same medial quality which is characteristic of simplicity in general. Idiom, too, is a plateau of generally equal elevation, though it may be interrupted by mountains or even volcanoes that rise above it, or by canyons that extend far below it. The English, Emerson says, are "perfect in the 'noble vulgar speech,' " in that kind of expression which, "though spoken among princes," is "equally fit and welcome to the mob."[241] Unbiased testimony to the merits of idiom as a usual abiding-place he finds in an un-

[239] *Natural History of Intellect: Art and Criticism*, 294.
[240] Ibid, 296.
[241] *English Traits: Literature*, 232.

expected quarter. He twice quotes no less a Latinist than Dr. Johnson to this effect: "There is in every nation a style which never becomes obsolete, a certain mode of phraseology so consonant to the analogy and principles of its respective language as to remain settled and unaltered. This style is to be sought in the common intercourse of life among those who speak only to be understood, without ambition of elegance. The polite are always catching modish innovations, and the learned forsake the vulgar, when the vulgar is right; but there is a conversation above grossness and below refinement, where propriety resides."[242]

Thus the idiomatic is standard, at least from an untranscendental point of view. It is satisfactory to the transcendentalist also. He considers it equally fit for expressing either the actual or the ideal or both in combination. Being of the soil it is never forgetful of hard fact. At the same time its closeness to Nature gives it, through its symbolic quality, remarkable spiritual values.

The idiomatic is accurate in expressing the actual because it is a part of Nature. The hunter or the miner "represents his facts as accurately as the cry of the wolf or the eagle tells of the forest or the air they inhabit."[243] In this sense his words are things. The idiomatic, accordingly, is obviously corporeal. Emerson notes with gladness that the English "delight in strong earthy expression, not mistakable, coarsely true to the human body. . . . This homeliness, veracity and plain style . . . imports into songs and ballads the smell of the earth, the breath of cattle, and, like a Dutch painter, seeks a household charm, though by pails and pans."[244]

Such a style, because of the vitality of its origin, has force. "Goethe said, 'Poetry here, poetry there, I have learned to speak German.' . . . And many of his poems are so idiomatic, so strongly rooted in the German soil, that they are the terror of translators, who say they cannot be rendered into any other language without loss of vigor, as we say of any darling passage of our own masters."[245]

Not only is the idiomatic of one piece with Nature; it is a part of human nature, of life and experience—and for this reason also accurate on the material plane. It deals only with essentials; it is absolutely untainted by literary affectation. Of Montaigne's writing Emerson says: "The sincerity and marrow of the man reaches to his sentences. I know not anywhere the book that seems less written. It is the language of conversation transferred to a book. Cut these words, and they would bleed; they

[242] Letters, *etc.: Eloquence*, 125–6. *Natural History and Intellect: Art and Criticism*, 284 (here printed without acknowledgment). This passage from Dr. Johnson is also quoted by A. B. Alcott (*Concord Days, April, Scholarship*). Alcott here, recommends the writing which is meditative, terse, and idiomatic.

[243] *Letters, etc.: Poetry and Imagination, Bards and Trouveurs*, 57.

[244] *English Traits: Literature*, 232.

[245] *Natural History of Intellect: Art and Criticism*, 284–5.

are vascular and alive."[246] "Montaigne must have the credit of giving to literature that which we listen for in bar-rooms, the low speech,—words and phrases that no scholar coined; street-cries and war-cries; words of the boatman, the farmer and the lord; that have neatness and necessity, through their use in the vocabulary of work and appetite, like the pebbles which the incessant attrition of the sea has rounded. Every historic autobiographic trait authenticating the man adds to the value of the book. We can't afford to take the horse out of the Essays; it would take the writer too."[247] "One has the same pleasure in" Montaigne's writing "that we have in listening to the necessary speech of men about their work, when any unusual circumstance gives momentary importance to the dialogue. For blacksmiths and teamsters do not trip in their speech; it is a shower of bullets. It is Cambridge men who correct themselves and begin again at every half sentence, and, moreover, will pun, and refine too much, and swerve from the matter to the expression."[248]

Emerson deplores the affected, jejune, unidiomatic style of review articles and other literary productions in which too much learning has caused a general juicelessness. He speaks thus of the scarcity of idiomatic writers in his day: "Our conventional style of writing is now so trite and poor, so little idiomatic, that we have several foreigners who write in our journals in a style not to be distinguished from their native colleagues."[249] He does not believe in linguistic proficiency as an aid to expression. "When I read," he declares, "of various extraordinary polyglots, self-made or college-made, who can understand fifty languages, I answer that I shall be glad and surprised to find that they know one. For if I were asked how many masters of English idiom I know, I shall be perplexed to count five."[250]

"Ought not," he asks, "the scholar to convey his meaning in terms as short and strong as the smith and the drover use to convey theirs? You know the history of the eminent English writer on gypsies, George Borrow; he had one clear perception, that the key to every country was command of the language of the common people. He therefore mastered the *patois* of the gypsies, called Romany, which is spoken by them in all countries where they wander, in Europe, Asia, Africa. . . . Bacon, if 'he could out-cant a London chirurgeon,' must have possessed the Romany under his brocade robes. Luther said, 'I preach coarsely; that giveth content to all. Hebrew, Greek and Latin I spare, until we learned ones come together, and then we make it so curled and finical that God himself

[246] *Representative Men: Montaigne,* 168.
[247] *Natural History of Intellect: Art and Criticism,* 295–6.
[248] *Representative Men: Montaigne,* 168.
[249] *Jour.* V, 215.
[250] *Natural History of Intellect: Art and Criticism,* 285.

wondereth at us.' He who would be powerful must have the terrible gift of familiarity,—Mirabeau, Chatham, Fox, Burke, O'Connell, Patrick Henry; and among writers Swift, De Foe, and Carlyle."[251]

The writer best succeeds who recognizes the material veracity of the idiomatic and combines it with high thinking to secure the desired duality; who, like Carlyle, "draws strength and mother-wit out of a poetic use of the spoken vocabulary, so that his paragraphs are all a sort of splendid conversation."[252] Emerson's advice is: "Speak with the vulgar, think with the wise. See how Plato managed it, with an imagination so gorgeous, and a taste so patrician, that Jove, if he descended, was to speak in his style. Into the exquisite refinement of his Academy, he introduces the low-born Socrates, relieving the purple diction by his perverse talk, his gallipots, and cook, and trencher, and cart-wheels—and steadily kept this coarseness to flavor a dish else too luscious."[253]

Emerson recognizes the dangers of this recommendation of low language. "Much of the raw material of the street-talk," he admits, "is absolutely untranslatable into print, and one must learn from Burke how to be severe without being unparliamentary. Rabelais and Montaigne are masters of this Romany, but cannot be read aloud, and so far fall short. Whitman is our American master, but has not got out of the Fire-Club and gained the *entrée* of the sitting-rooms."[254] Sublimation may be necessary before the idiomatic is fit for use. Burns was an adept at this kind of refining. "He had that secret of genius to draw from the bottom of society the strength of its speech, and astonish the ears of the polite with these artless words, better than art, and filtered of all offence through his beauty. It seemed odious to Luther that the devil should have all the best tunes; he would bring them into the churches; and Burns knew how to take from fairs and gypsies, blacksmiths and drovers, the speech of the market and street, and clothe it with melody."[255]

But there is another reason besides its materiality which causes the writer to avail himself of the popular speech. It has itself ideal values. In the first place, its material vitality makes it peculiarly fitted to the expression of the intense spiritually. Emerson notes in *English Traits* (*Ability*, 100) that "In Parliament, in pulpits, in theatres, when the speakers rise to thought and passion, the language becomes idiomatic; the people in the street best understand the best words." And he declares that "the idioms of all languages approach each other in passages of the greatest eloquence and power."[256] In the second place, the idiomatic, through its

[251] *Natural History of Intellect: Art and Criticism*, 285–6.

[252] *Jour*. IV, 196-7.

[253] *Natural History of Intellect: Art and Criticism*, 286–7.

[254] Ibid, 285–6.

[255] *Miscellanies: Robert Burns*, 442.

[256] *Nature, etc.: Language*, 29.

connection with Nature, is easily symbolic. "This immediate dependence of language upon nature, this conversion of an outward phenomenon into a type of somewhat in human life . . . gives that piquancy to the conversation of a strong-natured farmer or backwoodsman, which all men relish."[257]

In several of his own writings Emerson takes advantage of the symbolic quality of the idiomatic, and shows the philosophical or the spiritual in the colloquial. For example: "There is a little formula, couched in pure Saxon, which you may hear in the corners of streets and in the yard of the dame's school, from very little republicans: 'I'm as good as you be,' which contains the essence of the Massachusetts Bill of Rights and of the American Declaration of Independence."[258] The law of compensation he illustrates thus: "When I asked an ironmaster about the slag and cinder in railroad iron,—'O,' he said, 'there's always good iron to be had: if there's cinder in the iron it is because there was cinder in the pay.' "[259] The British dollars-and-cents attitude he discovers is that of "our unvarnished Connecticut question, 'Pray, sir, how do you get your living when you are at home?' "[260] The law of prudence is expressed, he believes, in the haymaker's advice: " 'Keep the rake . . . as nigh the scythe as you can, and the cart as nigh the rake.' "[261] He sees a lesson in optimism in "the sentiment of the poor woman who, coming from a wretched garret in an inland manufacturing town for the first time to the seashore, gazing at the ocean, said she was 'glad for once in her life to see something which there was enough of.' "[262] Of Carlyle's *Past and Present* he says: "It has the merit which belongs to every honest book, that it was self-examining before it was eloquent, and so hits all other men, and, as the country people say of good preaching, 'comes bounce down into every pew.' "[263]

The idiomatic also has a spiritual character through its connection with the theory of Each and All. The speech of common people represents close contact with experience, and every experience gives scope for a complete generalization—in this case all the more valuable because of the range from the mean fact to the spiritual law.

It is this universal extension to which the particular fact may be subjected that makes, for example, the argumentative value of what Emerson calls "the lowest classifying words . . . as, upstart, dab, cockney, prig, granny, lubber, puppy, peacock—'A cocktail House of Commons.' I remember when a venerable divine called the young preachers' sermon 'patty-cake.' The *sans-culottes* at Versailles cried out, 'Let our

[257] *Nature, etc.: Language*, 29.
[258] *Natural History of the Intellect: Boston*, 201.
[259] *Conduct of Life: Considerations by the Way*, 276.
[260] *English Traits: Ability*, 88.
[261] *Essays* I: *Prudence*, 235.
[262] *Letters, etc.: Resources*, 138–9.
[263] *Natural History of Intellect: Papers from the Dial, Past and Present*, 380.

little Mother Mirabeau speak!' "[264] "What argument, what eloquence can avail against the power of that one word *niggers*?"[265]

One kind of idiomatic classifying words of which Emerson is fond is nicknames. "No orator can measure in effect with him who can give good nicknames," he says.[266] He uses them so often himself that we wonder why he did not speak appreciation of the names which Dickens and Thackeray give their characters. We have already seen him characterizing the stupid man as Mr. Dunderhead. Mr. Grand and Mr. Hand make their appearance in *Spiritual Laws*[267] as delivering orations on the Fourth of July, the latter before the Mechanics' Association. Mr. Profitloss in *Power;*[268] Hotspur and Furlong in *Wealth;*[269] Mr. Curfew, Messieurs Turbinewheel, Summitlevel, and Lacofrupees in *Culture;*[270] Mr. Cockayne, the amateur farmer;[271] Mr. Hobnail, the reformer[272]—are some more rather ordinary examples. Truly delightful, however, are "Reverend Jul Bat, who has converted the whole torrid zone in his Sunday school; and Signor Torre del Greco, who extinguished Vesuvius by pouring into it the Bay of Naples";[273] and best of all Mr. Crump "with his grunting resistance to all his native devils."[274]

Idiomatic language, through its intimate connection with nature and experience, does the double work that Emerson demands of expression. With this in mind, it is not surprising to find him applying similar principles to the use of Saxon and Latin. In general he believed that "the short Saxon words with which the people help themselves are better than Latin," and preferred the Saxon, simpler, less pedantic words to the words of Latin derivation; *begin* for *commence*, *unfolding* for *development*, etc. "Be wary of the whole family of *Fero*,"[275] is his caution; *preference* he believed inferior to *choice*, *defer* to *give way*, *infer* to *gather*, *collate* to *bring together*, *translate* to *render*.

"One would," he asserts, "think the right use of words is almost lost who reads such a sentence as that of Lord Jeffreys to Richard Baxter, and compares it with our Latinized formulas. 'Richard, thou art an old knave; thou hast written books enough to load a cart; every one as full of

[264] *Natural History of Intellect: Art and Criticism*, 287.
[265] *Jour.* VII, 38.
[266] *Representative Men: Plato.*
[267] *Essays* I, 152.
[268] *Conduct of Life*, 82.
[269] Ibid, 124.
[270] Ibid, 157, 135.
[271] *Conduct of Life: Wealth*, 120.
[272] *Essays* II: *Manners*, 144.
[273] Ibid.
[274] *Essays* I: *Spiritual Laws*, 134.
[275] *Natural History of Intellect: Art and Criticism*, 292, 463–4.

sedition as an egg is full of meat. I know thou has a mighty party, and a great many of the brotherhood are waiting in corners to see what will become of their mighty Don; but by the grace of Almighty God, I'll crush you all.' "[276]

The Saxon word is likely to be more exact. It is short; it is close to life, experience and nature; it is language stripped, language which conveys only the bare essentials—and hence accurate, especially on a low plane. It is near kin to the actual thing even if it is not one with it. Unlike the word of Latin derivation, literary affectation has had no chance at it. The Latin word is at one remove from the thing it describes; and, as we shall see later in discussing compression and understatement, suffers from a tendency to excess, to inflation. On the other hand, the word of Latin derivation may often be accurate since it is directly allied to the higher and more abstract mental processes. Thus when properly blended with Saxon, it brings about the proper combination in expression of the physical and the metaphysical.

"In English," says Emerson, "only those sentences stand, which are good both for the scholar and the cabman, Latin and Saxon; half and half; perfectly Latin and perfectly English."[277] "It is a tacit rule of the language," he comments in *English Traits*,[278] "to make the frame or skeleton of Saxon words, and, when elevation or ornament is sought, to interweave Roman, but sparingly; nor is a sentence made of Roman words alone without loss of strength. The children and laborers," he observes, "use the Saxon unmixed. The Latin unmixed is abandoned to the colleges and Parliament. Mixture is a secret of the English island; and, in their dialect, the male principle is the Saxon, the female, the Latin; and they are combined in every discourse. A good writer, if he has indulged in a Roman roundness, makes haste to chasten and nerve his period by English monosyllables." "In all English rhetoric we use alternately a Saxon and a Roman word; often, two Saxon, but never willingly or wisely two Roman: e.g. 'A popular body of four hundred men.' 'A correct and manly debater.' "[279]

To be associated with Emerson's liking for the idiomatic is his fondness for popular forms of language which are in immediate touch with life and nature, and therefore satisfactory to both sense and spirit. The language of children, slang, the ungrammatical, profanity, and proverbs come in for a share of his approval.

Children's language comes close to the thing, and it is likely to be picturesque and symbolic, thus fulfilling the double requirement which

[276] *Jour.* IV, 304-5.
[277] *Jour.* VII, 561.
[278] *Literature*, 235.
[279] *Jour.* VIII, 421.

Emerson exacts. Their language is not a second-hand copy from books; it lives. Emerson asks: "What is so bewitching as the experiments of young children on grammar and language? The purity of their grammar corrects all the anomalies of our irregular verbs and anomalous nouns. They carry the analogy through. *Bite* makes *bited*, and *eat*, *eated*, in their preterite. Waldo says there is no 'telling' on my microscope, meaning no name of the maker, as he has seen on knife-blades, etc. 'Where is the wafer that *lives* in this box?' etc. They use the strong double negative which we English have lost from our books, though we keep it in the street. 'I wish you would not dig your leg,' said Waldo to me. Ellen calls the grapes 'green berries,' and when I asked, 'Does it rain this morning?' she said, 'There's tears on the window.' "[280]

We have previously seen that Emerson discovers the law of identity in variety revealed by the symbolic character of boyish slang. To the examples already given we may add some others in which he found the figurative element in slang interesting. "What can describe the folly and emptiness of scolding like the word *jawing*?"[281] "The collegians have seldom made a better word than 'squirt' for a showy sentence. . . . 'Honey-pie,' says State Street, when there is flattery; 'All my eye,' when any exaggeration."[282]

Slang and faulty grammar have strength to compensate for their lack of respectability. "Who has not heard in the street how forcible is bosh, gammon and gas. . . . I envy the boys the force of the double negative (no shoes, no money, no nothing)!"[283]

Grammatical errors are discoverable in Emerson's text, but his mistakes are rather of the nature of slips than defiantly intentional. Slang is almost wholly absent. I find but one dubious instance, this with the symbolic character so strong that the possibly base origin is entirely outgrown. The use of the word *gas* in the following is of particular interest since, as we have just seen, Emerson speaks of his enjoyment at hearing it "in the street." " 'Tis odd that our people should have not water on the brain, but a little gas there."[284]

Emerson's delight in profanity as a form of idiomatic speech is due to the esthetic and philosophical pleasure which he derives from it. He recognizes that under normal conditions it cannot with propriety enter into written expression, but at the same time he perceives its adequacy. It has life and vigor; in it, as in Carlyle's style, the "vicious conventions of writing are all dropped";[285] words are one with things. "This profane swearing

[280] *Jour.* V, 435.
[281] *Jour.* V, 419.
[282] *Jour.* VIII, 20.
[283] *Natural History of Intellect: Art and Criticism*, 287–8.
[284] *Conduct of Life: Culture*, 152.
[285] *Natural History of Intellect: Art and Criticism*, 297.

and bar-room wit has salt and fire in it,"[286] he declares; and thus describes its exactness and directness:

While Jake retorts and Reuben roars;
Scoff of yeoman strong and stark,
Goes like bullet to its mark;
While the solid curse and jeer
Never balk the waiting ear.[287]

"I confess to some pleasure," he says, "to some titillation of my ears, from the stinging rhetoric of a rattling oath in the mouth of truckmen and teamsters. How laconic and brisk it is by the side of a page of the North American Review! In the infinite variety of talents, 'tis certain that some men swear with genius. . . . What traveller has not listened to the vigor of the *Sacre!* of the French postilion, the *Sia ammazato!* of the Italian contadino, or the deep stomach of an English drayman's execration. I remember an occasion when a proficient in this style came from North Street to Cambridge and drew a crowd of young critics in the college yard, who found his wrath so aesthetic and fertilizing that they took notes, and even overstayed the hour of the mathematical professor."[288] "What a pity that we cannot curse and swear in good society! Cannot the stinging dialect of the sailors be domesticated? It is the best rhetoric, and for a hundred occasions those forbidden words are the only good ones. My page about 'Consistency' would be better written thus: Damn Consistency!"[289]

Sincere profanity satisfies as expression of the actual; indeed, Emerson's liking of it is the result of his perfect impartiality; his wish to recognize in the world of sense truth to fact in describing those things in which sense is absolutely unadulterated, his wish "to give even the Devil his due."[290] This is to be compared with his portrait of Mephistopheles in *Goethe*,[291] and with his remarks in another essay: "We were educated in horror of Satan, but Goethe remarked that all men like to hear him named. Burns took him into compassion and expressed a blind wish for his reformation.

Ye aiblins might, I dinna ken,
Still have a stake."—[292]

a wish in which, Emerson says, Plutarch would have joined. "And George Sand finds a whole nation who regard him as a personage who has been greatly wronged, and in which he is really the subject of a covert worship."[293]

[286] *Jour.* V, 420. Emerson objects, however, to immoderate, insincere oaths, "slam damns," *Jour.* VI, 236.

[287] *Poems: Monadnoc*, 66-7.

[288] *Jour.* V, 419 combined with *Natural History of Intellect: Art and Criticism*, 288.

[289] *Jour.* V, 484.

[290] *Lectures, etc.: Plutarch*, 299.

[291] *Representative Men*, 276-7.

[292] *Natural History of Intellect: Art and Criticism*, 289.

[293] Ibid.

Another reason for Emerson's pleasure in profanity is that he enjoys power wherever manifested, and strength as well as accuracy accompanies the swearing which is the result of genuine intensity of belief. Thus he quotes Lord Eldon as saying in his old age that " 'if he were to begin life again, he would be damned but he would begin as agitator' "[294]; and tells us that "In 1809, the majority in Parliament expressed itself by the language of Mr. Fuller in the House of Commons, 'If you do not like the country, damn you, you can leave it.' "[295]

Besides, profanity properly regarded is symbolic; it is a proof of Emerson's belief in the negative character of evil! "As a study in language, the use" of the word devil "is curious, to see how words help us and must be philosophical. The Devil in philosophy is absolute negation, falsehood, nothing; and in the popular mind, the Devil is a malignant person. Yet all our speech expresses the first sense. 'The Devil a monk was he,' means, *he was no monk*, and 'The Devil you did!' means *you did not*."[296]

Proverbs Emerson gives a high place. They are in all respects adequate expression. On the material side they satisfy because they are so instinct with life and its vigor, and because sage and long-continued experience gives vent in them to a happiness and finality of expression not otherwise to be attained.

On the spiritual side, too, they have great merit. They proceed from the character, and from the character, also, of not one man but many; from the *reason* of the universal man, that intellectual organ through which the Over-Soul speaks. They are "the statements of an absolute truth without qualification," "the sanctuary of the intuitions."[297] Thus they are exact expression on the highest level; in common with "words and grammar inflections" they "convey the public sense with more purity and precision than the wisest individual."[298]

And like all ideal expression, they are symbolic. Though some "have so the smell of current bank-bills that one seems to get the savor of all the marketmen's pockets,"[299] "there is no maxim of the merchant which does not admit of an extended sense, *e.g.*, 'Best use of money is to pay debts'; 'Every business by itself'; 'Best time is present time'; 'The right investment is in tools of your trade'; and the like. The counting-room maxims liberally expounded are laws of the universe."[300] Indeed, "that which the droning world, chained to appearances, will not allow the realist to say in his own words, it will suffer him to say in proverbs without contradic-

[294] *Essays* I: *Nominalist and Realist*, 284.
[295] *English Traits: Wealth*, 154.
[296] *Natural History of Intellect: Art and Criticism*, 289.
[297] *Essays* I: *Compensation*, 109.
[298] *Essays* II: *Nominalist and Realist*, 231.
[299] *Jour*. V, 35-6.
[300] *Conduct of Life: Wealth*, 125.

tion."[301] And it is true also that "the poor and the low have their way of expressing the last facts of philosophy as well as you. 'Blessed be nothing' and 'The worse things are, the better they are' are proverbs which express the transcendentalism of common life."[302]

Moreover, since proverbs are so entirely the result of experience, the law of Each and All applies to them with especial force. "Every homely proverb covers a single and grand fact. Two of these are often in my head lately: 'Every dog his day,' which covers this fact of otherism, or rotation of merits; and 'There are as good fish in the sea as ever came out of it'; which was Nelson's adage of *merit*, and all men's of *marriage*. My third proverb is as deficient in superficial melody as either of the others: 'The Devil is an ass.' The seamen use another which has much true divinity: 'Every man for himself and God for us all.' "[303]

As some of the quotations just given evidence, Emerson often took advantage of proverbs to support his doctrines. Other examples are to be found, in addition to further illustrations in the essays cited, in almost every essay in *Conduct of Life*, in *The Over-Soul*,[304] and in the lectures on *War* and *The Fugitive Slave Law*.[305]

Popular speech holds fast on life and nature, and therefore has in it all the qualities which Emerson desires in expression. In the field of either the actual or the ideal it is simple, sincere, pithy, direct, and strong; and it is exact because it is inseparable from the thing it describes. Its speakers have eyes which are keen and in focus; and they say what they see naturally, without damaging the value of their testimony through regard to bookish artificialities. Consequently out of the mouths of children, farmers, and blacksmiths proceedeth wisdom, for in telling the material facts of experience and nature as they see them they often utter spiritual truths; the actual being but the miniature counterfeit presentment of the ideal.

c. Compression

Many influences contribute toward Emerson's belief in compression as a quality of style. Most important, probably, is the nature of the man. Terseness has always marked the utterances of the wise man; and though many dispute Emerson's position as a philosopher, few deny that he is a sage, one of the Magi of all time. Such supermen or prophets or men of insight—names vary, though the phenomenon is similar—are famed not because of their connected discourse, but because of their pithy, universally wise sayings. "All mankind love a lover," "The only

[301] *Essays* I: *Compensation*, 109.
[302] *Essays* I: *Circles*, 315.
[303] *Jour.* V, 55-6.
[304] *Essays* I, 304.
[305] *Miscellanies*, 158, 194.

way to have a friend is to be one,"—through such apothegms as these the world knows Emerson. Rightly, for it is his whole tendency to wrap up his observations in neat, small packages. Like the other great prospectors of wisdom, he instinctively picks up from the sands of the river of truth nuggets of pure gold—handfuls only, but of exceeding price.

This native power is cousin to his propensity to tabulation. When his thoughts have continuity, he wishes them in convenient, portable, easily remembered form. He takes pleasure in boiling down a theory thus:

> Man puts things in a row;
> Things belong in a row;
> The showing of the true row is science.[306]

He is the expert advertiser or headline writer turned philosophical. His essays are frequently organized on the same principle. He numbers his points, in true ministerial style. After he has introduced a discussion in his *Journals*, he commands himself: "Come, then, count your reasons."[307]

Pedantry is not responsible for this tendency to enumeration. It is rather Emerson's desire to express himself adequately, to make words one with things. He counts that he may be sure of dealing only with things and not with mental shadows. By taking inventories frequently, he wards himself from the temptation to dispose of more stock then he really has on hand.

Compare with this attitude towards writing his parallel attitude toward its converse—reading. His point of view toward reading in general and philosophy in particular is not unlike that of the crammers in Owen Wister's classic college story, *Philosophy Four*. Says one of them in the midst of the process: " 'Oh, yes, Hobbes and his gang. There is only one substance, matter, but it doesn't strictly exist. Bodies exist. We've got Hobbes. Go on.' " Emerson likewise cared only for irreducible minima. He reckons the indispensable molecules in a book, and guided by this criterion, arrives at an estimate of its value. "I judge of a book," he says, ". . . by number and weight, counting the things that are in it."[308] This method he considers justified by the small number of thoughts that each book contributes. "They say," he writes, "that, though the stars appear so numberless, you cannot count more than a thousand. Well, there are few thoughts. Count the books and you would think there was immense wealth: but any expert knows that there are few thoughts which have emerged in his time. Shut him up in a closet, and he would soon tell them all. They are quoted, contradicted, modified, but the amount remains computably small."[309]

[306] *Jour.* IV, 60.
[307] *Jour.* IX, 217.
[308] *Jour.* IV, 23-4.
[309] *Jour.* IX, 134-5.

Emerson's policy toward reading is that of selection to the *nth* power. "I wish only to read," he says, "that which it would be a serious disaster to have missed."[310] In regard to the needlessness of a minute scrutiny of Platonic writers as a basis for understanding Platonism he inquires: "To know the flavor of tansy, must I eat all the tansy that grows by the wall?" It is "as if, to know the tree, you should make me eat all the apples. It is not granted to one man to express himself adequately more than a few times: and I believe fully . . . in interpreting the French Revolution by anecdotes, though not every diner-out can do it."[311] "Among our social advantages," he exclaims, "what a signal convenience is fame! Do we read all authors, to grope our way to the best? No; but the world selects for us the best, and we select from the best, our best."[312] And in these best books of ours, we select our sentences, or it may be, our words. "My debt to Plato," Emerson tells us, "is a certain number of sentences: the like to Aristotle. A larger number, yet still a finite number, make the worth of Milton and Shakspear to me."[313] " 'Tis really," he writes in his Journals later, "by a sentence or a phrase or two that many great men are remembered. Zoroaster has three or four, and Marcus Aurelius only as many."[314] And the extent of our debt "to every book that interests us" may be so low as "one or two words. Thus, to *Vestiges of Creation* we owe 'arrested development.' I remember to have seen three or four important words claimed as the result of Bentham, of which I think 'international' was one."[315]

So exacting a standard in regard to reading requires one of similar severity in regard to writing. The writer must avoid the fault of the Brook Farm reformers, who, Emerson says, "made it a rule not to bolt their flour, and unfortunately neglected also to sift their thoughts."[316] He may well anticipate the reader's process of selection. "The art of the writer is to speak his fact and have done. Let your reader find that he cannot afford to omit any line of your writing, because you have omitted every word that he can spare. You are annoyed—are you?—that your fine friends do not read you. They are better friends than you knew, and have done you the rarest service. Now write so that they must. When it is a disgrace to them that they do not know what you have said, you will hear the echo."[317]

[310] *Jour.* IX, 429.

[311] *Jour.* VIII, 44-5.

[312] *Jour.* VII, 53. Several pages in *Society and Solitude: Books* are to the same effect.

[313] *Jour.* IV, 23-4.

[314] *Jour.* X, 262.

[315] *Jour.* VII, 69-70.

[316] *Jour.* VI, 475.

[317] *Jour.* IX, 436-7.

Adopting the reader's point of view and saving him the trouble of picking out essentials makes for expression which is adequate—in the realm of either actual or ideal—because vital, spontaneous, exact. "All writing," Emerson asserts, "should be selection in order to drop every dead word. Why do you not save out of your speech or thinking only the vital things,—the spirited *mot* which amused or warmed you when you spoke it,—because of its luck and newness? I have just been reading, in this careful book of a most intelligent and learned man, any number of flat conventional words and sentences. If a man would learn to read his own manuscript severely,—becoming really a third person, and search only for what interested him, he would blot to purpose,—and how every page would gain! Then all the words will be sprightly, and every sentence a surprise."[318] In writing, as Hesiod says, "the half is better than the whole." Or, as Boileau's neat French phrase has it, "The secret of boring you is that of telling all." If we are going to write truly, we must blot resolutely. "Resolute blotting rids you of all those phrases that sound like something and mean nothing. . . . As soon as you read aloud, you will find what sentences drag. Blot them out, and read again, you will find the words that drag."[319]

Compression is important whether the writer is expressing the material or the spiritual. For the former purpose its advantages are obvious. Because of its exactness, it saves time. Commendable "frugality" of this sort Emerson sees in Goethe, where "you shall find no word that does not stand for a thing."[320]

That condensation makes for accuracy on a low plane is shown also by the effect on language of those who use it as a necessity and not as a literary luxury: "See how children build up a language; how every traveller, every laborer, every impatient boss who sharply shortens the phrase or the word to give his order quicker, reducing it to the lowest possible terms, and there it must stay,—improves the national tongue."[321] Working of the same tendency is apparent in the economical exactness of the idiomatic; of the Saxon element in English, for example. Children's language has a like merit: "What is so weak and thin as our written style to-day in what is called literature? We use ten words for one of the child's. His strong speech is made up of nouns and verbs, and names the facts."[322]

In the literature of the ideal compression is even more necessary than in that of the actual. " 'Tis inexcusable in a man who has messages to men, who has truths to impart, to scribble flourishes. He should write

[318] *Jour.* X, 303.

[319] *Natural History of Intellect: Art and Criticism*, 291.

[320] *Natural History of Intellect: Papers from the Dial, Thoughts on Modern Literature*, 323.

[321] *Letters, etc.: Resources*, 140.

[322] *Jour.* V, 435.

that which cannot be omitted; every sentence a cube, standing on its bottom like a die, essential and immortal. When cities are sacked and libraries burned, this book will be saved,—prophetic, sacred, a book of life."[323]

In poetry, consequently, compression is to be carried farther than in prose. For though prose may be ideal in content, poetry must be. Rhyme and rhythm, as well as lofty symbols, are unmistakable indications of the altitude of poetry and make necessary a difference in its material from that of prose. It carries selection of substance much farther. Prose "selects only the eminent experiences; Poetry, the supereminent."[324] Hence Emerson says that "In reading prose, I am sensible as soon as a sentence drags, but in reading poetry, as soon as one word drags."[325] The poet, to a far greater extent than the prose-writer, must "omit all but the important passages. Shakspeare is made up of important passages, like Damascus steel made up of old nails."[326] Poetry is peculiarly the result of inspiration, and "the inexorable rule in the muses' court, *either inspiration or silence*, compels the bard to report only his supreme moments. It teaches the enormous force of a few words, and in proportion to the inspiration checks loquacity."[327]

Compression, furthermore, is characteristic of ideal style because such expression must be symbolic or suggestive rather than direct. Those who came to Emerson seeking advice on moral questions worked out their own answers, his habit being not to reply expressly but to stimulate the inquirer to a right solution by speaking of parallel matters or in general terms. Such is the case with everything partaking of the nature of the divine: we see God in the burning bush rather than face to face. "God himself does not speak prose, but communicates with us by hints, omens, inference and dark resemblances in objects lying all around us."[328] Knowing this, the writer chooses the concise style in his attempts to convey the spiritual. Since not what is said but what is hinted is important he leaves to the reader the creative pleasure of supplying "the unsaid part" which is "the best of every discourse."[329] Thus it is that "the silences, pauses, of an orator are as telling as his words;"[330] and that in written discourse suppression may do more to convey the high thought than any number of words. By their absence, words make noble thought perspicuous as well as conspicuous.

[323] *Jour.* IX, 423.
[324] *Jour.* VII, 517.
[325] *Jour.* IX, 214.
[326] *Letters, etc.: Poetry and Imagination, Veracity*, 33.
[327] Ibid, *Transcendency*, 72-3.
[328] Ibid, *Poetry*, 12.
[329] *Jour.* III, 492.
[330] *Natural History and Intellect: Art and Criticism*, 290.

The limitations to which language is subject account in large measure for the fact that conciseness marks the ideal expression. Even when we understand spiritual truths, we still find them incommunicable. They "refuse to be adequately stated." The roundness and completeness which characterize the ideal thought, words, which are detached particles, can never satisfactorily represent. "The moral traits which are all globed into every virtuous act and thought,—in speech we must sever, and describe or suggest by painful enumeration of many particulars."[331] And when our spiritual perceptions are weak, the impulse to heap up details in the effort to achieve an ineffable whole is all the stronger. "In proportion as a man's life comes into union with truth," Emerson declares, "his thoughts approach to a parallelism with the currents of natural laws, so that he easily expresses his meaning by natural symbols, or uses the ecstatic or poetic speech. . . . In proportion as his life departs from this simplicity, he uses circumlocution,—by many words hoping to suggest what he cannot say."[332] These being the difficulties, it is plain that correction must come by avoiding the leaning toward verbosity which is the sign of weakness, and by using the one apt symbolic phrase which is most largely implicative.

In connection with compression as a quality of spiritual expression, there should be mentioned another cause operating in Emerson's case to make him favor this quality. This was his disgust at the unmeaning prolixity of the sermons of his day. "But the minister in these days," Emerson complains, "—how little he says! Who is the most decorous man? and no longer, who speaks the most truth? Look at the orations of Demosthenes and Burke, and how many irrelevant things, sentences, words, letters, are there? Not one. Go into one of our cool churches, and begin to count the words that might be spared, and in most places the entire sermon will go. One sentence kept another in countenance, but not one by its own weight could have justified the saying of it. 'Tis the age of Parenthesis. You might put all we say in brackets and it would not be missed."[333] Better was the practice of the Concord sage, the Rev. Ezra Ripley. "The structure of his sentences was admirable; so neat, so natural, so terse, his words fell like stones; and often, though quite unconscious of it, his speech was a satire on the loose, voluminous, draggle-tail periods of other speakers."[334] Emerson records his pleasure, too, on an occasion when "Rev. Phillips Brooks offered a prayer, in which not a word was superfluous, and every right thing was said."[335]

[331] *Nature, etc.: Address*, 121-2.

[332] *Letters, etc.: Poetry and Imagination, Morals*, 68.

[333] *Jour.* III, 549.

[334] *Lectures, etc.: Ezra Ripley, D. D.*, 392.

[335] *Jour.* X, 333.

Emerson found ministers particularly prone to use sterotyped phrases, phrases which should be omitted because they do not stand for things. He shares Coleridge's aversion to the insincere (because individually unthought and unfelt) expression fallen into by the preacher who believes that the words of the Bible are the only inspired and hence the only fit ones for religious uses. He asserts that if he made laws for a divinity school, he would "gazette every Saturday all the words they were wont to use in reporting religious experience, as 'spiritual life,' 'God,' 'soul,' 'cross,' etc., and if they could not find new ones next week, they might remain silent."[336] And in general, he objects to making literature "a sum in the arithmetical rule, permutation and combination."[337] "I hope the time will come," he says, "when . . . it will be unpardonable to say, 'the times that tried men's souls,' or anything about 'a cause,' "[338] or " 'the Good and the True.' "[339]

Besides religious and philosophical words which have been "used up," " a list might be made of showy words that tempt young writers:" and have likewise been done to death; "*asphodel, harbinger, chalice, flamboyant, golden, diamond, amethyst, opal* and the rest of the precious stones, *carcanet, diadem.*"[340]

Not only the words which have become fossilized through too frequent use by others, but those which we ourselves favor to excess are objectionable. Sainte-Beuve speaks of the fondness of writers for certain words, and of the clue this furnishes to their ruling passion or fixed idea. (Perhaps Holmes[341] got the hint from Sainte-Beuve to interpret Emerson by his favorite words, which he says are *haughty, fine,* and *melioration.*) Similarly, Emerson says that "Persons have been named from their abuse of certain phrases, as 'Pyramid' Lambert, 'Finality' Russell, 'Humanity' Martin, 'Horizon' Turner."[342] E. P. Whipple[343] tells of a conversation in which he remarked on Emerson's frequent use of the word *grim.* "Do you say I use the word often?" asked Emerson in some alarm. "The word is probably passing with me into a mannerism, and I must hereafter guard against it,—must banish it from my dictionary."

Emerson's advocacy of compression should also be considered in relation to the Each and All theory, and with regard to his methods of organization as connected with that theory. Since the whole truth resides in any part of the truth, his effort is to write short sentences, which as John

[336] *Jour.* VI, 525.
[337] *Jour.* III, 549.
[338] Ibid.
[339] *Natural History of Intellect: Art and Criticism,* 293.
[340] Ibid.
[341] *Ralph Waldo Emerson,* 404-5.
[342] *Natural History of Intellect: Art and Criticism,* 293.
[343] *Recollections of Eminent Men: Some Recollections of Ralph Waldo Emerson,* 127.

Burroughs says of proverbs, "give us pocket-editions of the most voluminous truths."[344] Such sentences have an independent value and possibilities of independent existence apart from their context. Emerson often writes sentences which he himself calls "infinitely repellent particles," but which may be more accurately described as he describes those of Landor: "Of many of Mr. Landor's sentences we are fain to remember what was said of those of Socrates; that they are cubes, which will stand firm, place them how or where you will."[345]

Emerson's accidental discovery of the individual merit of the sentences in his first book is told thus in his Journals: "To-day came to me the first proof-sheet of *Nature* to be corrected, like a new coat, full of vexations; with the first sentences of the chapters perched like mottoes aloft in small type! The peace of the author can not be wounded by such trifles, if he sees that the sentences are still good. A good sentence can never be put out of countenance by any blunder of compositors. It is good in text or note, in poetry or prose, as title or corollary. But a bad sentence shows all his flaws instantly by such dislocation. So that a certain sublime serenity is generated in the soul of the poet by the annoyances of the press. He sees that the spirit may infuse a subtle logic into the parts of the piece which shall defy all accidents to break their connection."[346]

Emerson, then, favors the "solid" sentence, in which "you can even spare punctuation," since the place of the word "in the sentence should make its emphasis."[347] Carlyle, he notes approvingly, "crowds meaning into all the nooks and corners of his sentences. Once read, he is but half read."[348]

The epitaph in Boswell's Johnson "on the criminal who was killed by a fall from his horse" is excellent:

> Between the stirrup and the ground
> I mercy asked and mercy found.

For "which word can you spare, what can you add?"[349]

But such praise of the solid sentence does not mean that compression is to be confounded with "an obscure, elliptical style." There is a wide difference between them. "A good writer must convey the feeling of a flamboyant witness, and at the same time of chemic selection,—as if in his densest period was no cramp, but room to turn a chariot and horses. . . . In good hands," compression "will never become sterility," for "the dense writer has yet ample room and choice of phrase, and even a

[344] *Expression.*
[345] *Natural History of Intellect: Papers from the Dial, Walter Savage Landor,* 349.
[346] *Jour.* IV, 81-2.
[347] *Jour.* III, 272.
[348] *Jour.* IV, 196.
[349] *Jour.* IV, 268.

gamesome mood often between his valid words. There is no inadequacy or disagreeable contraction in his sentence, any more than in a human face, where in a square space of a few inches is found room for every possible variety of expression. There must be no cramp insufficiency, but the superfluous must be omitted. In the Hindoo mythology, 'Viswaharmán' placed the sun on his lathe to grind off some of his effulgence, and in this manner reduced it to an eighth,—more was inseparable."[350]

Though Emerson's sentences are compressed, it has been charged with some justice that all his ideas are presented in *Nature*, and the two series of *Essays*, and that later work is merely amplification and repetition. Emerson was aware of this criticism, and acknowledged its possible validity. "Why do I write another line," he asks, "since my best friends assure me that in every line I repeat myself?"[351] "Captain Franklin," he says in an earlier passage in the Journals, "after six weeks' traveling to the North Pole on the ice, found himself two hundred miles south of the spot he set out from: the ice had floated. And I sometimes start to think I am looking out the same vocables in the Dictionary, spelling out the same sentences, solving the same problems.—My ice may float also."[352]

Professor Firkins[353] goes even farther than this. Not only in different books, but in the same essay, even in the same paragraph, he finds repetition. However condensed the sentences, individually considered, may be, a multitude of examples illustrating one main thought are sometimes grouped to make an essay, as in *History*.[354] Every compartment in the sample-case is snugly packed, but every one holds a sample of the same kind of commodity.

The incongruities of the situation are to a considerable extent explained by the Each and All theory. Emerson delights in seeing the oak in any one acorn; but at the same time he is by so much more pleased when he sees the phenomenon repeated in a great variety of instances. Thus the same theory gives rise to the apparent contradiction of compression in the sentences, and repetition in the larger units.

One other aspect of interrelationship between the methods of constructing sentences and of building up paragraphs and sentences needs to be spoken of. This is the unfortunate effect of lack of clearness in progression of the thought caused, on the one hand, by the attempt to secure condensation in the sentence, and, on the other hand, by Emerson's disbelief in too obvious transition. The sentence which is con-

[350] *Natural History of Intellect: Art and Criticism* combined with *Papers from the Dial, Walter Savage Landor*, 290-1 and 348.

[351] *Jour.* VI, 73.

[352] *Jour.* III, 460.

[353] *Ralph Waldo Emerson.*

[354] *Essays* I.

structed so that it may stand alone has a tendency to find this isolation, though juxtaposed to other sentences expressing part of the same general line of thought. And dispensing with transition results both in obscurity and in an increasing of the aphoristic effect. Thus Emerson's strength and his weakness meet.

There is still to be mentioned another influence contributing toward Emerson's belief in compression. This is its artistic quality. "The line of beauty is the result of perfect economy. . . . 'It is the purgation of superfluities,' said Michael Angelo. . . . This art of omission is a chief secret of power, and, in general, it is proof of high culture to say the greatest matters in the simplest way."[355] This is a Greek ideal, and Emerson recognized it as such. "Access to the Greek mind," he says, "lifts" the Englishman's "standard of taste. . . . The great silent crowd of thoroughbred Grecians always known to be around him, the English writer cannot ignore. They prune his orations and point his pen."[356] In explaining the small number of entries in the Journal for 1860, Dr. Edward Emerson tells us that "This was due to Mr. Emerson's occupation of severely pruning and refining for his book, *Conduct of Life*, the lectures which, as delivered, had much matter to hold the attention of Lyceum audiences in the country at large. Mrs. Emerson remonstrated, missing good anecdotes and lighter touches, but her husband answered, 'No, we must put on their Greek jackets for the book.' "[357]

In theory and in practice, of course, Emerson recognizes exceptions to this rigid requirement of omission. The man whose range of thought and expression is wide has a right to fluency and plenteousness of style. Such a man was Rabelais. "The style at once decides the high quality of the man. It flows like the river Amazon, so rich, so plentiful, so transparent, and with such long reaches, that longanimity or longsightedness which belongs to the Platos. No sand without lime, no short, chippy, indigent epigrammatist or proverbialist with docked sentences, but an exhaustless affluence."[358]

"How remarkable," also, "the principle of iteration in rhetoric! We are delighted with it in rhyme, in poetic prose, in song, above all, allowing a line to be not only a burden to the whole song, but, as in negro melodies, to be steadily repeated three or four times in immediate succession. Well, what shall we say of a liturgy? what of a litany? what of a Lord's Prayer, the burial service, which is echoed and reechoed from one end of man's life to the other."[359] Carlyle knew this principle. He "is full of rhythm, not

[355] *Conduct of Life: Beauty*, 294.
[356] *English Traits: Universities*, 207.
[357] *Jour.* IX, 287 Note.
[358] *Jour.* VI, 279.
[359] *Jour.* IX, 447.

only in the perpetual melody of his periods, but in the burdens, refrains, and grand returns of his sense and music."[360] "This trick of rhyme, burden, or refrain, which he uses so well, he not only employs in each new paragraph, suddenly treating you with the last *ritornello*, but in each new essay or book quoting the Burden or Chorus of the last book—you know me, and I know you; or, Here we are again; come take me up again on your shoulders,—is the import of this."[361] Examples of the effective use of repetition Emerson finds also in the Bible, " 'At her feet he bowed, he fell, he lay down: at her feet he bowed, he fell: where he bowed, there he fell down dead.' The fact is made conspicuous, nay, colossal, by this simple rhetoric:—'They shall perish but thou shalt endure: yea, all of them shall wax old like a garment; as a vesture shalt thou change them, and they shall be changed: but thou art the same, and thy years shall have no end.' "[362]

To this collection of examples should be added Emerson's own use of the refrain at the end of *Fate* in *Conduct of Life*. "Let us build altars to the Beautiful Necessity," sounds majestically at intervals in the midst of the gloria which brings the essay to a grand finale.

But usually, in the effort to use as simple means as possible, Emerson seeks a style which exactly fills the mould of its thought. He is led to it, in part, by his seerlike tendency to aphorism and by his recognition of the artistic beauty of economy. Equally important considerations are the value of compression in expressing either the material or the ideal or both; and its help in making the sentence which, though in the narrowest limits, incloses divinity. Disposition and theory unite, then, to make it Emerson's aim to bound in a nutshell the thing of infinite space.

d. Understatement and the Superlative

Two tendencies in Emerson's style and his theories about style fight one another constantly, and only truces of compromise and mutual adjustment make possible even intermittent peace between them. One is his desire for intensity of expression, his wish to represent unrestrained his intimations of immortal thought. The other tendency is his determination to express himself accurately, each word standing for a clearly embodied entity. The conflict comes from the fact that emotion recollected in tranquillity and examined analytically cannot be uttered with its original fervor. Each part may be enunciated distinctly and precisely, but the penalty for such adequacy in the expression of the parts is likely to be inadequacy in expression of the whole. The fusing heat has forever escaped and been lost.

[360] *Natural History of Intellect: Papers from the Dial, Past and Present*, 391.
[361] *Jour.* VIII, 95.
[362] *Letters, etc.: Poetry and Imagination, Melody, Rhyme, Form*, 47.

Often, but as we shall see not always, Emerson finds his *via media* in the twofold value of that expression in which the superlative is avoided, even at the risk of understatement. In presentation of the everyday fact it is obvious that accuracy demands the shunning of exaggeration. At the same time in expression of the ideal, mildness, reticence, implication that much more could be said, have an effect stimulating, suggestive, symbolic—are often far more powerful, indeed, than an undammed Niagara of emotion.

Emerson noted on his trip to Italy that the "Italians use the superlative too much. . . . A man, to tell me that this was the same thing I had before, said, 'È l'istessissima cosa'; and at the *trattoria*, when I asked if the cream was good, the waiter answered, 'Stupendo!' "[363] Another Latin race, the French, suffers from the same habit of linguistic inflation. Under the heading of *The Gallic Cock* the Journals contain the following: "An errand boy in France is *commissionaire;* a kitchen is *laboratoire;* applied to is *consacrée.*"[364] But this fault, inexact use of the superlative, is not confined to the Italians and French. "We talk, sometimes, with people whose conversation would lead you to suppose that they had lived in a museum, where all the objects were monsters and extremes. Their good people are phoenixes; their naughty are like the prophet's figs. They use the superlative of grammar: 'most perfect,' 'most exquisite,' 'most horrible.' Like the French, they are enchanted, they are desolate, because you have got or have not got a shoe-string or a wafer you happen to want,—not perceiving that superlatives are diminutives, and weaken; that the positive is the sinew of speech, the superlative the fat. If the talker lose a tooth, he thinks the universal thaw and dissolution of things has come. Controvert his opinion and he cries 'Persecution!' and reckons himself with Saint Barnabas, who was sawn in two.

". . . 'Tis very wearisome, this straining talk, these experiences all exquisite, intense and tremendous,—' the best I ever saw;' 'I never in my life!' One wishes these terms gazetted and forbidden. Every favorite is not a cherub, nor every cat a griffin, nor each unpleasing person a dark, diabolical intriguer; nor agonies, excruciations nor ecstacies our daily bread."[365]

People who use such terms are uncivilized, uncultured; their intelligence is insufficiently developed and their powers of expression are correspondingly limited so that they are driven to vehemence in the vain effort to convey their ideas. They see things in "lumps and masses" rather than "accurately distributed," and like children "cry, scream and stamp with fury, unable to express" themselves. The grown up individual or

[363] *Jour.* III, 120.
[364] *Jour.* VII, 457.
[365] *Lectures, etc.: The Superlative*, 163-5.

race puts away childish things, and speaks as a man. Plato is thus superior to preceding philosophers: he "needs no barbaric paint, or tattoo, or whooping; for he can define. He leaves with Asia the vast and superlative; he is the arrival of accuracy and intelligence."[366]

Accuracy in expression, whether of the actual or the ideal, demands a much closer approach to the fact than the hit-or-miss superlative makes possible. Those "unskilful definers" who "from want of skill to convey quality, . . . hope to move admiration by quantity," are doomed to disappointment. "Language should aim to describe the fact. It is not enough to suggest it and magnify it. Sharper sight would indicate the true line. . . . The first valuable power in a reasonable mind" is "the power of plain statement, or the power to receive things as they befall, and to transfer the picture of them to another mind unaltered. 'Tis a good rule of rhetoric which Schlegel gives,—'In good prose, every word is underscored;' which, I suppose, means, Never italicize."[367]

Another cause working towards the necessity of caution in expression is the character of language. Every part of nature by virtue of its relation to the pervading unity is a rounded whole. Yet the multitude and unbounded distribution of these units makes it difficult for the writer to speak of any one without neglecting the others. Language cannot, with entire success, imitate nature's ability to tell the whole truth in a particle. "Every sentence hath some falsehood of exaggeration in it. For the infinite diffuseness refuses to be epigrammatized, the world to be shut in a word. The thought being spoken in a sentence becomes by mere detachment falsely emphatic."[368] "It is the fault of our rhetoric that we cannot strongly state one fact without seeming to belie some other."[369] Hence there is all the more need of certainty that things be presented as they are, without strain, swelling, or distortion.

Furthermore, though nature sets the writer an impossible task, it gives by its own practice a hint of the desirability of measure in writing, especially in expression of the actual. "In nature there is no emphasis."[370] "Nature measures her greatness by what she can spare, by what remains when all superfluity and accessories are shorn off."[371] "Nature never swears, loves temperate expressions and sober colors, green grass, fawns and drabs, greys and blues and dark mixed; now and then a grim Acherontian fungus."[372]

[366] *Representative Men: Plato*, 45-47.
[367] *Lectures, etc.: The Superlative*, 164, 168-9.
[368] *Jour.* VI, 65.
[369] *Essays* I: *History*, 39.
[370] *Jour.* VI, 35.
[371] *Lectures, etc.: The Superlative*, 174.
[372] *Jour.* VI, 236.

Consequently it is not surprising that those who live close to nature and actualities and partake thereby of its characteristics refrain from excess in their expression. The farmer, for instance, has not the literary man's inclination towards "inflation," that "disease incident to too much use of words." He speaks only things, and is careful not to speak more things than his keenly discerning eyes see. "I am daily struck," Emerson declares, "with the forcible understatement of people who have no literary habit. The low expression is strong and agreeable. . . .

"The common people diminish: 'a cold snap;' 'it rains easy;' 'good haying weather.' When a farmer means to tell you that he is doing well with his farm, he says, 'I don't work as hard as I did, and I don't mean to.' When he wishes to condemn any treatment of soils or of stock, he says, 'It won't do any good.' Under the Catskill Mountains the boy in the steamboat said, 'Come up here, Tony; it looks pretty out-of-doors.' The farmers in the region do not call particular summits, as Killington, Camel's Hump, Saddleback, etc., mountains, but only 'them 'ere rises,' and reserve the word mountains for the range."[373]

There is a similar proneness to understatement in the work of those authors whose gaze is fixed primarily on the common details of life and experience. Montaigne, for instance, "uses the positive degree; never shrieks, or protests, or prays: no weakness, no convulsion, no superlative; does not wish to jump out of his skin, or play any antics, or annihilate space or time, but is stout and solid. . . . He keeps the plain; he rarely mounts or sinks; likes to feel solid ground and the stones underneath."[374] Webster's oratory was marked by a like nearness to fact. Emerson records in his Journals that he "clings closely to the business part of his speech with great gravity and faithfulness. 'I do not inflame,' he said on one occasion, 'I do not exaggerate; I avoid all incendiary allusion.' He trusts to his simple strength of statement."[375] "He hugs his fact . . . close, and will not let it go, and never indulges in a weak flourish, though he knows perfectly well how to make such exordiums and episodes and perorations as may give perspective to his harangue, without in the least embarrassing his plan or confounding his transitions. What is small, he shows as small, and makes the great, great."[376]

Most of the advantages of the positive degree so far set down relate particularly to its value in expressing the actual. But in expression of the ideal, too, the positive degree, or even understatement, has a place, perhaps the place. We have only to recall Emerson's belief that "the unsaid part is the best of every discourse" to see why restrained language is strong

[373] *Lectures, etc.: The Superlative*, 169-70.
[374] *Represenatative Men: Montaigne*, 169.
[375] *Jour.* VI, 342.
[376] *Jour.* VI, 432.

language, for it hints at far more than it utters, and has a kind of symbolic significance much greater than its immediate denotation. "Doctor Channing's piety and wisdom," Emerson tells us, "had such weight that, in Boston, the popular idea of religion was whatever this eminent divine held. But I remember that his best friend, a man of guarded lips, speaking of him in a circle of his admirers, said: 'I have known him long, I have studied his character, and I believe him capable of virtue.' An eminent French journalist paid a high compliment to the Duke of Wellington, when his documents were published: 'Here are twelve volumes of military dispatches, and the word *glory* is not found in them.' "[377]

And when the language of the ideal is direct rather than suggestive, it is still characterized by plain and unadorned simplicity. Emerson believes with Madame de Staël: "Surely all that is simple is sufficient for all that is good."[378] For the men who speak divine truth can do so only because of their own simplicity and absence of pretension. They know that God's voice speaks through them, and that their manner of expression, even what they say, is of no importance compared to the eternal soul in whose messages they share. Hence, even at the risk of seeming "frigid and phlegmatic to those who have been spiced with the frantic passion and violent coloring of inferior but popular writers," "they use the positive degree." They know that nothing will serve in heavenly matters save "casting aside . . . trappings and dealing man to man in naked truth, plain confession and omniscient affirmation."[379]

In spite of this utter absence of show and display in the writing of the genuine idealist, idealists have certain enemies who, by copying what they believe to be the mannerisms of the idealists' language, strive to be mistaken for them, and to gain credit for virtue, though they have it not. Such persons, "seeing that the sentiments please, counterfeit the expression of them. These we call sentimentalists,—talkers who mistake the description for the thing, saying for having. They have, they tell you, an intense love of Nature; poetry,—O, they adore poetry,—and roses, and the moon, and the cavalry regiment, and the governor; they love liberty, 'dear liberty!' they worship virtue, 'dear virtue!' Yes, they adopt whatever merit is in good repute, and almost make it hateful with their praise. The warmer their expressions, the colder we feel; we shiver with cold."[380]

Politics and religion are particularly infested by these false counterparts. In the *Speech on Affairs in Kansas*[381] Emerson thus exposed the sham in the words of the slavery advocates: "Language has lost its meaning in the

[377] *Lectures, etc.: The Superlative*, 166-7.
[378] *Jour.* IV, 163.
[379] *Essays* I: *The Over-Soul*, 288-9, 291.
[380] *Letters, etc.: Social Aims*, 105.
[381] *Miscellanies*, 259-60.

universal cant. *Representative Government* is really misrepresentative; *Union* is a conspiracy against the Northern States which the Northern States are to have the privilege of paying for; the *adding of Cuba and Central America* to the slave marts is *enlarging the area of Freedom. Manifest Destiny, Democracy, Freedom,* fine names for an ugly thing. They call it otto of rose and lavender,—I call it bilge-water. They call it Chivalry and Freedom; I call it the stealing all the earnings of a poor man and the earnings of his little girl and boy, and the earnings of all that shall come from him, his children's children forever."

As for the superficial would-be doubles in religious matters: "What," asks Emerson, "is so odious as the polite bows to God, in our books and newspapers? The popular press is flagitious in the exact measure of its sanctimony, and the religion of the day is a theatrical Sinai, where the thunders are supplied by the property-man."[382] And with these pretenders in mind, the sincerely religious person will make himself as unlike them as possible. If they use sacred names hypocritically, he will use them only when he must. "You cannot say *God, blood* and *hell* too little. Always suppose God. The Jew named him not."[383]

As much to be avoided as the pinchbeck and overdone protestations of nobility is the contrary habit of descending to laud what is really unpraiseworthy. Historians especially Emerson finds subject to this fault; sometimes in the midst of otherwise lofty work he sees them kowtowing to the insignificant. He objects to Bancroft's "insertion of a boyish hurrah, every now and then, for each State in turn, which resembles the fortune of the good professor in Mathematics in a Southern College, who was not permitted to go on with his exercise on Election Day without interposing in his demonstration, ABF=GHI, Hurrah for Jackson! and so on."[384] More serious is the case when "Histories are written, like this Forster's (Cromwell), in ridiculous deference to all the lowest prejudices. The simple fact of being the potentate of England seems to the good scribe a thing so incredible and venerable that he can never allude to it without new astonishment and never records a victory without new bows and duckings and *empressements*."[385]

The positive degree is safe; it is exact; it may even be intense. The actual demands bare and precise expression; and the soul's messages shun grandiloquence. "Spartans, stoics, heroes, saints and gods use a short and positive speech."[386] Yet it would not be fair to say that the duplex satisfaction attained by careful repression is always agreeable to Emerson

[382] *English Traits: Religion*, 229.
[383] *Jour.* VII, 101.
[384] *Jour.* IV, 304.
[385] *Jour.* V, 262-3.
[386] *Lectures, etc.: The Superlative*, 169.

in either theory or practice. True, he was capable of uttering what to the orthodox of his day seemed heresies, in a disarming, innocent, unconcerned way: witness the Divinity College *Address*.[387] He wreaks destruction without crying Havoc! and his dogs of war are trained not to bay. But it is just as much the fact that he sometimes lets loose the reins. Pegasus is not always bridled; he sometimes spurns the middle road, soars above and away from it, goeth where he listeth. It may be that the sincere mood is strong and will vent itself, scorning the danger that an equally sincere contrary mood may demand cool adjudication by the impartial. It may be that exaggeration will serve a humorous purpose. Or it may be that the richly stored mind discloses its wealth in a gorgeous bazaar of infinitely varied treasures. In such cases, Emerson believes going to extremes justifiable.

The first of these situations brings up the often-mooted question of Emerson's inconsistency, which many have fastened on him as a stigma, though he himself would consider the charge the highest praise. In his opinion only through inconsistency in the details is consistency in the wholes possible. The many-sided truth can never be altogether realized or expressed unless all its parts in turn are glorified by the person enthusiastic about the merits of each part. "If one would study his own time, it must be by this method of taking up in turn each of the leading topics which belong to our scheme of human life, and by firmly stating all that is agreeable to experience on one, and doing the same justice to the opposing facts in the others, the true limitations will appear. Any excess of emphasis on one part would be corrected, and a just balance would be made."[388] Emerson's defense of Carlyle in this regard equally fits his own practise, and incidentally points out the danger involved in this kind of superlative. "Like all men of wit and great rhetorical power, he is by no means to be held to the paradox he utters to-day. He states it well, and overstates it, because he is himself trying how far it will bear him. But the novelty and luster of his language makes the hearers remember his opinion, and would hold him to it long after he has forgotten it."[389] It is to forestall this misconception that Emerson issues the plain warning: "Lest I should mislead any when I have my own head and obey my whims, let me remind the reader that I am only an experimenter. Do not set the least value on what I do, or the least discredit on what I do not, as if I pretended to settle any thing as true or false. I unsettle all things. No facts are to me sacred; none are profane; I simply experiment, an endless seeker with no Past at my back."[390]

[387] *Nature, etc.*
[388] *Conduct of Life: Fate*, 4.
[389] *Jour.* VII, 367.
[390] *Essays*, I: *Circles*, 318.

This investigating spirit, with its disposition to strong and even intense expression of its momentary enthusiastic and unchecked appreciation of value, Emerson supports no matter if the result seems to be overpraise of material things. For though misconstruction of such eulogy of the lower things may seem to constitute an assault on virtue, virtue cannot thereby be hurt. "Some of my friends have complained," says Emerson in beginning his essay on *Worship*,[391] ". . . that we discussed Fate, Power and Wealth on too low a platform; gave too much line to the evil spirit of the times; too many cakes to Cerberus; that we ran Cudworth's risk of making, by excess of candor, the argument of atheism so strong that he could not answer it. I have no fears of being forced in my own despite to play as we say the devil's attorney. I have no infirmity of faith; no belief that it is of much importance what I or any man may say: I am sure that a certain truth will be said through me, though I should be dumb, or though I should try to say the reverse. Nor do I fear skepticism for any good soul. A just thinker will allow full swing to his skepticism. I dip my pen in the blackest ink, because I am not afraid of falling into my inkpot. I have no sympathy with a poor man I knew, who, when suicides abounded, told me he dared not look at his razor. We are of different opinions at different hours, but we always may be said to be at heart on the side of truth."

In this case, as in all such, overstatement has the advantage that it makes possible the eventual telling of the whole truth. "If the Divine Providence has hid from men neither disease nor deformity nor corrupt society, but has stated itself out in passions, in war, in trade, in the love of power and pleasure, in hunger and need, in tyrannies, literatures and arts,—let us not be so nice that we cannot write these facts down coarsely as they stand, or doubt but there is a counter-statement as ponderous, which we can arrive at, and which, being put, will make all square."[392]

The superlative may serve justifiably another purpose, that of humor. "The superlative, so dreary in dull people, in the hands of wit gives a fillip or shock most agreeable to the attention, and hints at poetic power."[393] The "weak and wearisome lie" is "very different . . . from the stimulus to the fancy which is given by a romancing talker who does not mean to be exactly taken,—like the gallant skipper who complained to his owners that he had pumped the Atlantic Ocean three times through his ship on the passage, and 'twas common to strike seals and porpoises in the hold. Of what was similarly asserted of the late Lord Jeffrey, at the Scottish bar,—an attentive auditor declaring on one occasion after an argument of three hours, that he had spoken the whole English language three times

[391] *Conduct of Life*, 201.

[392] *Conduct of Life: Worship*, 202.

[393] *Jour.* IX, 499.

over in his speech."[394] Examples of this kind of exaggeration occur in Emerson's own writing when he hits at the narrow sectarians who, as he says, "dress up that terrific benefactor [Providence] in a clean shirt and white neckcloth of a student in divinity;"[395] and when he tells us that the scientist "has got all snakes and lizards in his phials, but science has done for him also, and has put the man into a bottle."[396]

Emerson, finally, has some praise for those writers whose breadth of intellect was such as to give them the right to use the style which is adorned, exuberant, or even violent, though he finds "few specimens of" such "magnificence. Plato is the purple ancient, and Bacon and Milton the moderns of the richest strains. Burke sometimes reaches to that exuberant fulness, though deficient in depth."[397] "Clarendon alone among the English authors (though I think I see the love of Clarendon in Burke) has successfully transplanted the Italian superlative style."[398] "Carlyle, in his strange, half-mad way, has entered the Field of the Cloth of Gold, and shown a vigor and wealth of resource which has no rival in the tourney-play of these times;—the indubitable champion of England."[399]

Emerson, however, was never quite satisfied that the extravagance and vehemence of Carlyle's style was altogether pardonable or necessary. He does see palliations, of course. "You will say," he writes to Carlyle, "no rules for the illumination of windows can apply to the Aurora borealis."[400] And he makes the excuse for Carlyle that "in all his fun of castanets, of playing of tunes with a whiplash like some renowned charioteers, —in all this glad and needful venting of his redundant spirits, he does yet, ever and anon, as if catching the glance of one wise man in the crowd, quit his tempestuous key, and lance at him in clear, level tone the very word, and then with new glee return to his game. He is like a lover or an outlaw who wraps up his message in a serenade, which is nonsense to the sentinel, but salvation to the ear for which it is meant."[401] But more often his attitude is in consonance with what we have discovered to be his central position with regard to style; simplicity in all expression, whether of the actual or the spiritual. "There is the Periclean and there is the Slam-bang style. O Carlyle, the merit of glass is not to be seen, but to be seen through; but every crystal and lamina of the Carlyle glass is visible."[402] And in more direct apostrophe, Emerson delivered himself thus: "I

[394] *Lectures, etc.: The Superlative*, 171-2.
[395] *Conduct of Life: Fate*, 8.
[396] *Conduct of Life: Beauty*, 284.
[397] *Natural History of Intellect: Papers from the Dial, Past and Present*, 389-90.
[398] *Jour.* IV, 269.
[399] *Natural History of Intellect: Papers from the Dial, Past and Present*, 390.
[400] *C. E. Corr.* I, 131.
[401] *Natural History of Intellect: Papers from the Dial, Past and Present*, 389.
[402] *Jour.* VII, 216.

comprehend not why you should lavish in that spendthrift style of yours celestial truths. . . . I look for the hour with impatience when the vehicle will be worthy of the spirit,—then the word will be as simple, and so as resistless, as the thought,—and, in short, when your words will be one with things."[403]

There are occasions when precision gives way to an ecstasy which "plays with all the works of Nature, great or minute, galaxy or grain of dust, as toys and words of the mind;"[404] when the enthusiastic emotion overleaps the hurdles of caution; when humor scorns the nice fact; when the wealthy in mind are generous with their expression. But adequacy comes more often through the simple positive speech, which is one with things whether seen or unseen, temporal or eternal.

To clothe the fiery thought
In simple words succeeds,
For still the craft of genius is
To mask a king in weeds.[405]

[403] *C. E. Corr.* I, 14-15.
[404] *Lectures, etc.: The Superlative*, 176.
[405] *Poems*, 292.

METHOD

During a lecture in England, one of Emerson's hearers, it is said, leaned over to his neighbor and inquired, "What's the connection?" "There is none, save in God," was the answer. This reply is excellent criticism of the structure of Emerson's essays. It finds fault justly: if the connection is divine, our yearning to know what it is should be satisfied. And with censure, the reply mingles due praise. It is, after all, much that the connection should be in God: this would hardly be the case but for the fact that the thoughts requiring connection are themselves holy.

Such lack of obvious relationship as is pointed to by the anecdote is due to Emerson's belief in the dualism inherent in transcendentalism. The truths which his Reason perceives, beyond consciousness and experience, have a connection in God which it is difficult for mortal eye to see constantly and completely, and which it is all the more difficult to express. Yet for Emerson merely earthly connection, transition for transition's sake, will not suffice in such cases. Here then, is an important effect of dualism on Emerson's method of writing. There are other results, too, proceeding from the general division between the seen and the unseen; and from its corollary doctrine of Each and All, which is determinant in matters affecting organization because it concerns itself with the relation of spiritual integers to detached earthly fractions.

To see definitely how these conceptions affect Emerson's ideas with regard to structure in literary composition, especially his own, it is necessary in the first place to take into account his Journals and note what influences exerted themselves there on his methods of writing.

Even before he had reached sixteen he began the keeping of a literary diary or commonplace book. His first purpose was simply that of gaining practice in writing and of collecting from other writers passages pleasing by reason of their matter or manner. Gradually this became joined with a vague intention of gathering the wisdom of his age through both quotation and original presentation of current ideas. A strong youthful admiration for Bacon and for his experimental philosophical method, especially as applied to morals, suggested to Emerson the possibility of thus taking as his own province contemporary philosophical knowledge. In May 1824, at the age of 21, he had gone far enough in consideration of this life aim, to set down in his Journals his emulous hope. After mentioning as examples Pope's *Moral Essays* and *Essay on Man,* the Proverbs of Solomon, and Montaigne's Essays (which he had not yet read) he says as modestly as the circumstance permitted: "I am not so foolhardy as to write *Sequel to Bacon* on my title-page; and there are some reasons that induce me to suppose that the undertaking of this enterprise does not imply any censurable arrogance. . . . It may be made clear that there may be the Wisdom of an Age, independent of and above the Wisdom of any individual whose life is numbered in its years. And the diligence rather than the genius of one mind may compile the prudential maxims, domestic and public maxims current in the world and which may be made to surpass the single stores of any writer, as the richest private funds are quickly exceeded by a public purse."[1]

This ambition continued through Emerson's life, but in a modified form. For soon the humble gatherer of other men's opinions acquired self-reliance. The trust company combined its affairs with a "Savings Bank,"[2] which accumulated miscellaneous wealth subject only to the test that it be genuine currency fresh every day from the Emersonian mint. Many causes helped to bring this about. The voices of Channing, Coleridge, Carlyle and—through the latter two—Kant and Goethe proclaimed that the voice of God could still be heard, and that inspiration was still possible; and thus encouraged both religious and literary independence. Emerson's indomitably individual Aunt Mary did much in the same direction by precept and example. And his own withdrawal from the church and trip to Europe, with accompanying disappointment at celebrities whom he met, completed the work of emancipation.

These influences are important, but they perhaps do not so directly affect the contents of the Journals as another influence which has never received its full credit, that of Montaigne. "In Roxbury, in 1825," Emerson tells us, "I read Cotton's translation of Montaigne. It seemed to me as if I had written the book myself in some former life, so sincerely it spoke my thought and experience. No book before or since was ever so much to me as that."[3] It seems more than likely that thus, the next year after Emerson heralded his intention of bringing together all contemporary copybook knowledge, Bacon partly gave way to a new hero, a hero whose example stimulated him to a paradoxical but real mixture of self-reliance, desire to imitate, and desire to excel. Montaigne, like Bacon, has the spirit of inquiry; but his inquiry is personal and based on individual experience. His preface makes this clear enough to most readers, and probably made it clear to Emerson. In regard to him, Emerson wrote to his Aunt Mary in 1831: "No effeminate parlor workman is he on an idea got at an evening lecture or a young men's debate, but roundly tells what he saw or what he thought of when he was riding on horseback or entertaining a troop at his château."[4] And, with more

[1] *Jour.* I, 392-3.
[2] *Jour.* III, 246.
[3] *Jour.* VI, 372-3.
[4] *Representative Men*, 336.

spirituality, this is precisely what Emerson was at this time gaining confidence to do; so that the Journals become more and more the record of high daily inspiration meekly received—in recognition of what Emerson considered its divine source—but boldly imparted. That Emerson regarded himself as a follower of Montaigne, though with a difference, a significant passage in the Journals in 1835 bears witness. In it he enumerates his stock of ideas, and reminds himself of his intention of writing essays. And he begins with this question: "When will you mend Montaigne?"[5] He, too, wishes to use his own experiences, thoughts, and feelings as the substance of his writings; but for a higher, holier purpose.

The father of the essay was also the father of Emerson's essays. But Bacon, the father of the English essay, has almost paternal claims on them. The impulse which Bacon had fostered still survived; Emerson still wished to assemble "a cumulative moral and intellectual science." In 1835 he shows by a record in the Journals that the hope of eleven years before was yet alive. "By and by," he says, "books of condensed wisdom may be writ by the concentrated lights of thousands [of] centuries which shall cast Bacon and Aristotle into gloom."[6] A change has come in this purpose only in the fact that now his contribution is to be self-derived or at least self-tested. The continuance of his aim, thus modified, is shown in the course of lectures which he delivered at Harvard in 1870, later published under the title, *Natural History of Intellect.*

The change, however, has an important effect on his literary procedure. Whatever might have been the chance for regulated homogeneity otherwise, by keeping Bacon's experimental method and joining with it the recording of personal "anecdotes of the intellect," writing "a sort of Farmer's Almanac of mental moods"[7] he prevents himself from ever arriving at a philosophical system. And in the same way he makes it difficult to arrive at organization and continuity in the essays which collect these anecdotes. We shall see later how much he wished to avoid this difficulty; but how, when it proved insuperable, he found some reasons for being contented with his endless dotting, as he described it.

Thus both Bacon and Montaigne had their share in influencing the organization of Emerson's essays. In cooperation with the impersonal but strong aid of the Each and All theory, Bacon affects it in two other even more definite ways. The first of these needs little more than mention. Emerson's paragraphs, as Professor Firkins has pointed out, often hold together well because they have the parallelism which results from his habit of collecting examples or symbolic illustrations of a dominating principle; and the same is true even of some of the essays. It is easy to see how

[5] *Jour.* III, 480.
[6] *Jour.* III, 518-9.
[7] *Natural History of Intellect: Powers and Laws of Thought,* 11.

this habit is itself caused by joining emulation of Bacon's inductive method with the wish to show identity in variety.

But Bacon suggested to Emerson something of far more importance than the value of psychological generalization. He had a spiritual as well as a scientific influence. Compilation of such data is not enough; to be truly of worth they must be seen in the light of the universal laws which govern them. Ignorance of these laws is ignorance of the real import of the individual facts. Furthermore, these universal principles are not empirical; though they serve a deductive, classifying purpose, they are major premises which have been realized intuitively and not through laborious experiment. Such premises belong to what Bacon called the First Philosophy. Bacon, says Emerson in his chapter on *Literature* in *English Traits*, "required in his map of the mind, first of all, universality, or *prima philosophia;* the receptacle for all such profitable observations and axioms as fall not within the compass of any of the special parts of philosophy, but are more common and of a higher stage. He held this element essential: . . . believing that no perfect discovery can be made in a flat or level, but you must ascend to a higher science. . . He explained himself by giving various quaint examples of the summary or common laws of which each science has its own illustration. . . Plato had signified the same sense, when he said, 'All the great arts require a subtle and speculative research into the law of nature, since loftiness of thought and perfect mastery over every subject seem to be derived from such source as this.' " In the Journals, in 1830, Emerson writes that Bacon's *prima philosophia* is "that generalization which gives the elevation to all the writings of Burke, of De Staël, and now of Sampson Reed."[8]

The alignment of the *prima philosophia* with ideal dualism is plain. Indeed, as early as 1835 Emerson had defined the *prima philosophia* as "the science of what is, in distinction from what appears."[9] The Reason only is capable of seeing and uttering the laws of the First Philosophy; for they are supersensuous, the lofty principles which pervade and unite the messages of the Over-Soul. Plato and the Platonists have enunciated most of them. "In England these may be traced usually to Shakspeare, Bacon, Milton, or Hooker, even to Van Helmont and Behmen, and do all have a kind of filial retrospect to Plato and the Greeks."[10]

The relation between the *prima philosophia* and the scattered facts to which it gives meaning is, furthermore, not very different from the relation between the One and the Many, between All and Each, to use Emerson's nomenclature. According to this, too, particular facts are valuable

[8] *Jour.* II, 331. Emerson's Swedenborgian friend, of whom more is said in the chapter on The Growth of Emerson's Theories of Style.

[9] *English Traits*, 380.

[10] *English Traits: Literature*, 241.

only as spiritual units illuminate them. Once more, Bacon and the Each and All theory join hands.

Both the effect of dualism on writing, and Emerson's belief that an author's noblest aim should be to make his own contribution to the First Philosophy, come out plainly in a letter to Carlyle written in 1859. After expressing his gratification at what Carlyle has already done in literature, he says: "Yet that book will not come which I most wish to read, namely, the culled results, the quintessence of private conviction, a *liber veritatis*, a few sentences, hints of the final moral you drew from so much penetrating inquest into past and present men. All writing is necessitated to be exoteric, and written to a human *should* instead of to the terrible *is*. . . Every writer is a skater, who must go partly where he would, and partly where the skates carry him; or a sailor, who can only land where sails can be safely blown. The variations to be allowed for in the surveyor's compass are nothing like so large as those that must be allowed for in every book." But, Emerson goes on to say, "passion for euphony, and surface harmonies, and tenderness for . . . accidental literary stores" are as nothing compared to what a writer has to say "touching the problems of man and fate and the Cause of Causes. . . So," he finishes, "if ever I hear that you have betrayed the first symptom of age . . . I shall hasten to believe that you are shearing your prodigal overgrowths and are calling your troops to the citadel, and I may come in the first steamer to drop in of evenings and hear the central monosyllables."[11]

The conceptions of the *prima philosophia* and of Each and All, as well as ideal dualism in general, have important effects on Emerson's theory and practice with regard to compositional structure. It is desirable, however, to preface consideration of these with some discussion of Emerson's problem of organization, and of his artistic theories regarding method and unity in writing.

From the Journals came all the Works, so that it was Emerson's task, as he tells Carlyle, "to spin some single cord out of my thousand and one strands of every color and texture that lie ravelled around me in old snarls."[12] Paragraphs, even sentences, written years apart, were pieced together in the completed essays. Any such method must have its grave limitations; continuity and unity of tone and thought are difficult, if not impossible, to achieve under such conditions. Yet comparison of the Journals with the essays shows that the patchworking process has been remarkably successful considering the number and variety of pieces in the completed quilts. Such a careful and discriminating reader as Professor Firkins asserts that "method, in some form or degree, is universal in Emerson." (p. 238.)

[11] *C. E. Corr.* II, 264-5.
[12] *C. E. Corr.* I, 282.

Indeed, it would be strange if this were not the case. For in theory, at least, there is no doubt that Emerson was fully aware of and believed in the most artistic kind of coherence, unity, and proportion. It is true that in his search for adequacy of expression, he kept close to the bird of his thought while it was on the wing, and without stopping it in its flight, recorded the very notes of its song. Yet he did not hesitate, when the connection of thoughts set down in his journals at different times became clear to him, to join these related ideas. "Let not a man," he says, "decline being an artist under any greenhorn notion of intermeddling with sacred thought. It is surely foolish to adhere strictly to the order of time in putting down one's thoughts, and to neglect the order of thought. I put like things together."[13] "The art of writing consists in putting two things together that are unlike and that belong together, like a horse and cart. Then have we somewhat far more goodly and efficient than either."[14]

Unity and proportion, too, Emerson regarded as of prime importance in writing as in other forms of art, for "Art, in the artist, is proportion, or a habitual respect to the whole by an eye loving beauty in details."[15] He approves of "Couture's rule of looking three times at the object, for one at your drawing . . . and William Hunt's emphasis, after him, on the mass, instead of the details! And how perfectly . . .," he exclaims, "the same rule applies in rhetoric or writing!"[16] "It is well and truly said," is his comment elsewhere, "that proportion is beauty; that no ornament in the details can compensate for want of this; nay, that ornamented details only make disproportion more unsightly; and that proportion charms us even more perhaps when the materials are coarse and unadorned. I see these truths chiefly in that species of architecture which I study and practice, namely, Rhetoric, or the Building of Discourse. Profoundest thoughts, sublime images, dazzling figures are squandered and lost in an immethodical harangue. We are fatigued, and glad when it is done. We say of the writer, Nobody understood him: he does not understand himself. But let the same number of thoughts be dealt with by a natural rhetoric, let the question be asked—What is said? How many things? Which are they? Count and number them: put together those that belong together. Now say *what your subject is*, for now first you know: and now state your inference or peroration in what calm or inflammatory temper you must, and behold! out of the quarry you have erected a temple, soaring in due gradation, turret over tower, to heaven, cheerful with thorough-lights, majestic with strength, desired of all eyes."[17]

[13] *Jour.* IV, 246.
[14] *Jour.* IV, 483.
[15] *Essays* II: *Nominalist and Realist,* 234.
[16] *Jour.* X, 335.
[17] *Jour.* IV, 335-6.

Emerson's attitude toward artistic organization comes out interestingly in his attitude toward *ex tempore* speeches. Though he yearned all his life for the intensity which would fuse thoughts and words and make unprepared delivery possible, he almost never trusted himself to such inspiration. And from the esthetic point of view he saw great advantages in preparation. "Extempore speaking can be good, and written discourses can be good," he says. "A tent is a very good thing, but so is a cathedral."[18] In the speech on *The Assault on Mr. Sumner* he says: "And the third crime he stands charged with, is, that his speeches were written before they were spoken; which, of course, must be true in Sumner's case, as it was true of Webster, of Adams, of Calhoun, of Burke, of Chatham, of Demosthenes; of every first-rate speaker that ever lived. It is the high compliment he pays to the intelligence of the Senate and of the country. When the same reproach was cast on the first orator of ancient times by some caviler of his day, he said, 'I should be ashamed to come with one unconsidered word before such an assembly.' "[19]

Could Emerson recognize lack of artistic organization when he met with it? He found deficient in this respect Landor, Bacon, Goethe, and Milton. Landor "has not the high, overpowering method by which the master gives unity and integrity to a work of many parts."[20] Bacon's work "is fragmentary, wants unity. It lies along the ground like the materials of an unfinished city."[21] Of Goethe, he says: "This lawgiver of art is not an artist. Was it that he knew too much, that his sight was microscopic and interfered with the just perspective, the seeing of the whole? He is fragmentary; a writer of occasional poems and of an encyclopædia of sentences. When he sits down to write a drama or a tale, he collects and sorts his observations from a hundred sides, and combines them into the body as fitly as he can. A great deal refuses to incorporate: this he adds loosely as letters of the parties, leaves from their journals, or the like. A great deal still is left that will not find any place. This the bookbinder alone can give any cohesion to; and hence, notwithstanding the looseness of many of his works, we have volumes of detached paragraphs, aphorisms, *Xenien*, etc."[22] On Milton's prose writings, the *Areopagitica* excepted, he has this comment to make: "Their rhetorical excellence must also suffer some deduction. They have no perfectness. These writings are wonderful for the truth, the learning, the subtility and pomp of the language; but the whole is sacrificed to the particular. Eager to do fit justice to each thought, he does not subordinate it so as to project the main argument.

[18] *Jour.* V, 236.

[19] *Miscellanies: The Assault upon Mr. Sumner*, 250-1.

[20] *Natural History of Intellect: Walter Savage Landor*, 348.

[21] *Memoir* II, 720.

[22] *Representative Men: Goethe*, 287-8.

He writes whilst he is heated; the piece shows all the rambles and resources of indignation, but he has never *integrated* the parts of the argument in his mind. The reader is fatigued with admiration, but is not yet master of the subject."[23]

In this illustrious company of weaklings, Alcott may be introduced if only to show that this kind of frailty affects the small as well as the great. "The *Post* expresses the feeling of most readers in its rude joke, when it said of his *Orphic Sayings* that they 'resembled a train of fifteen railroad cars with one passenger.' "[24]

Perhaps the surest test of Emerson's critical ability in regard to method is his attitude toward his own delinquencies. He is his own severest critic. It is he who makes the unjust charge that he writes "paragraphs incompressible, each sentence an infinitely repellent particle."[25] He uses many clever metaphors to describe his weakness. After speaking of his tendency to "the lapidary style," he says: "I build my house of boulders; somebody asked me 'if I built of medals.' "[26] He writes again to Carlyle: "I get a brick-kiln instead of a house."[27] "I found," he confesses to himself, "when I had finished my new lecture that it was a very good house, only the architect had unfortunately omitted the stairs."[28] He is as modest in his public writing: "In our present attempt to enumerate some traits of the recent literature, we shall have somewhat to offer on each of these topics, but we cannot promise to set in very exact order what we have to say."[29] "I shall attempt in this and the following chapter to record some facts that indicate the path of the law of Compensation; happy beyond my expectation if I shall truly draw the smallest arc of this circle."[30] "I know better," he says in *Experience*,[31] "than to claim any completeness for my picture. I am a fragment, and this is a fragment of me. I can very confidently announce one or another law, which throws itself into relief and form, but I am too young yet by some ages to compile a code. I gossip for my hour concerning the eternal politics."

He does not, however, merely acknowledge this weakness and find consolation in conviction of futility. He prays for improvement. "If Minerva offered me a gift and an option," he writes, "I would say give me continuity. I am tired of scraps. I do not wish to be a literary or intellectual chiffonier. Away with this Jew's rag-bag of ends and tufts of

[23] *Natural History of Intellect: Milton*, 249.
[24] *Jour.* VI, 171.
[25] *C. E. Corr.* I, 161.
[26] *C. E. Corr.* I, 345.
[27] *C. E. Corr.* I, 299.
[28] *Jour.* VIII, 167.
[29] *Natural History of Intellect: Papers from the Dial, Thoughts on Modern Literature*, 311.
[30] *Essays* I: *Compensation*, 96.
[31] *Essays* II, 83.

brocade, velvet, and cloth-of-gold; let me spin some yards or miles of helpful twine, a clew to lead to one kingly truth, a cord to bind wholesome and belonging facts.

> The Asmodæan feat be mine
> To spin my sand heaps into twine."[32]

It is certain that Emerson wished to show the relations of the parts of his writings to each other and their relation to the whole. The difficulty was that for him the whole is the Unity which governs the universe. In this broad sense, he desired to make clear the relation of the particular to the universal, but he did not always feel certain that he knew what that relation was. Concerning definitions he says that they can be hoped for "only from a mind conversant with the First Philosophy. . . Mr. Landor's definitions are only enumerations of particulars; the generic law is not seized."[33] Emerson had a mind conversant with the First Philosophy, but he did not always feel certain that he had seized the generic law. The *prima philosophia* and the Each and All theory thus affect his organization. For in matching passages from his diary, though he was sure that the passages belonged to the same subject, he was not always sure of the connection between them. Rather than put in a false, superficial connection, he preferred to put in none. His failure to organize his compositions more lucidly is, then, due to the same cause as his failure to erect what, in any sense, may be called a system of philosophy. He found little beauty or utility in a chain of which some of the links, though speciously as firm as the others, are really only alloy makeshifts to hold together the links of pure metal. His lack of organization results not from inability as far as giving the appearance of method was concerned, but from his unwillingness to group things in a certain order when he was not confident that it was, in the highest sense, the right one.

If, on the other hand, he had been able to arrange his ideas in such form as to bring out their true connection with each other, there is no doubt that he would gladly have done so. He believed that the power to organize truly and not merely with ingenuity was one of the marks of genius: "There is a certain momentum of mass which I recognize readily enough in literature," he declares. "Chaucer affects me when I read many pages of . . . the *Canterbury Tales* by his mass, as much as by the merit of single passages. So does Shakspeare eminently: he adds architecture to costliness of material, and beauty of single chambers and chapels. So does Milton. Then, as I have remarked of Pythagoras, so I feel in reference to all great masters, that they are chiefly distinguished by their power of adding a second, a third, and perhaps a fourth step in a continuous line. Many

[32] *Jour.* VIII, 463.
[33] *Natural History of Intellect: Walter Savage Landor*, 346.

a man had taken their first step. With every additional step you enhance immensely the value of your first. It is like the price which is sometimes set on a horse by jockeys; a price is agreed upon in the stall, and then he is turned into a pasture and allowed to roll, and for every time he shall roll himself over, ten dollars are added to the price."[34]

One and only one kind of philosophical system satisfies Emerson: that which is all-inclusive and that which rests firmly on dualism, which has as its wellspring the First Philosophy. Rounded system is desirable, but it is hard to attain. "Nothing is more carefully secured in our constitution than that we shall not systematize or integrate too fast. Carry it how we will, always something refuses to be subordinated and to drill. It will not toe the line. The facts of animal magnetism are now extravagant. We can make nothing of them. What then? Why, own that you are a tyro. We make a dear little cosmogony of our own that makes the world, and tucks in all nations like cherries into a tart,—and 'tis all finished and rounded into compass and shape; but unluckily we find that it will not explain the existence of the African race."[35] And in another passage Emerson says: "I confess to a little distrust of that completeness of system which metaphysicians are apt to affect. 'Tis the gnat grasping the world. All these exhaustive theories appear indeed a false and vain attempt to introvert and analyze the Primal Thought. That is upstream, and what a stream! Can you swim up Niagara Falls?"[36]

Only the idealist has any chance of avoiding this difficulty. "Every fact studied by the Understanding is not only solitary but desart. But if the iron lids of Reason's eye can be once raised, the fact is classified immediately and seen to be related to our nursery reading and our profoundest science."[37] "It will not do for Sharon Turner, or any man not of Ideas to make a System. Thus, Mr. Turner had got into his head the notion that the Mosaic history is a good natural history of the world, reconcilable with geology, etc. Very well. You see at once the length and breadth of what you may expect, and lose all appetite to read. But Coleridge sets out to idealize the actual, to make an *epopœa* out of English institutions, and it is replete with life."[38] And Plato, though his "vision is not illimitable," nevertheless "codifies and catalogues and distributes" so that "in his broad daylight things reappear as they stood in the sunlight, hardly shorn of a ray, yet now portable and reportable."[39]

What is true of philosophy is likewise true of writing. The author who "works . . . in the spirit of a cabinet-maker, rather than that of an archi-

[34] *Jour.* VI, 155-6.
[35] *Jour.* IV, 294.
[36] *Natural History of Intellect: Powers and Laws of Thought*, 12.
[37] *Jour.* III, 539.
[38] *Jour.* III, 567.
[39] *Jour.* VIII, 44-45.

tect" presents "the thought which strikes him as great and Dantesque, and opens an abyss . . . transformed into a chamber or a neat parlor." He lacks the necessary universal grasp, and thus "degrades ideas."[40] History has usually been written by such inefficient writers. "Let us learn," Emerson urges, "with the patience and affection of a naturalist all the facts, and looking out all the time for the reason that was, for the law that prevailed, and made the facts such; not for one that we can supply and make the facts plausibly sustain. . . Why should not history be godly written, out of the highest Faith and with a study of what really was? We should then have Ideas which would command and marshal the facts, and show the history of a nation as accurately proportioned and necessary in every part as an animal."[41]

According to Emerson's definition, classicism is but another name for the kind of executive power which is caused by vision of controlling ideal principles. "The classic unfolds: the romantic adds," he says, discriminating between the appearance of organization and the real thing. Classicism sees all facts and incidents and thoughts as but offshoots of a high and life-giving central purpose. Eugène Sue and Dumas he considers by this test romantic; Scott (in one novel) and Shakspeare (in at least one play) classic. The first two "when they begin a story, do not know when it will end; but Walter Scott when he began the *Bride of Lammermoor* had no choice, nor Shakspeare in *Macbeth*." And he considers that "George Sand, though she writes fast and miscellaneously, is yet fundamentally classic and necessitated: and I," he says, "who tack things strangely enough together, and consult my ease rather than my strength, and often write *on the other side*, am yet an adorer of the *One*."[42]

The ideal system must, of course, be genuine, and it is Emerson's advice to "Shun manufacture, or the introducing and artificial arrangement in your thoughts—it will surely crack and come to nothing."[43] What, then, are to be the actions of the writer who is seeking the high kind of unity which Emerson advocates? What, especially, is the writer to do who keeps a diurnal record of thoughts just as they happen to occur to him? How is he to get "high enough above" his materials "to see their order in reason" and to be able to "manage or dispose?"[44] His problem and his right course of action Emerson thus outlines: "There is a process in the mind very analogous to crystallization in the mineral kingdom. I think of a particular fact of singular beauty and interest. In thinking of it I am led to many more thoughts which show themselves, first partially, and

[40] *Jour.* VI, 74.
[41] *Jour.* V, 66.
[42] *Jour.* IX, 25.
[43] *Jour.* III, 550.
[44] *Jour.* II, 520.

afterwards more fully. But in the multitude of them I see no order. When I would present them to others they have no beginning. There is no method. Leave them now, and return to them again. Domesticate them in your mind, do not force them into arrangement too hastily, and presently you shall find they will take their own order. And the order they assume is divine. It is God's architecture."[45] And to the same effect he says in another passage: "Any single fact considered by itself confounds, misleads us. Let it lie awhile. It will find its place, by and by, in God's chain; its golden brothers will come, one on the right hand and one on the left, and in an instant it will be the simplest, gladdest, friendliest of things."[46]

Writing so organized, in the "natural order," as Emerson calls it, will prove the most satisfactory to writer and reader. "If a natural order is obediently followed, the composition will have an abiding charm to yourself as well as to others; you will see that you were the scribe of a higher wisdom than your own, and it will remain to you, like one of Nature's works, pleasant and wholesome, and not, as our books so often are, a disagreeable remembrance to the author."[47]

Not only must the system have a divine origin, but its means of connection must also be spiritual, truly representative of high thinking. Of Landor Emerson says that "what skill of transition he may possess is superficial, not spiritual."[48] And in general he declares that "a continuous effect cannot be produced by discontinuous thought, and when the eye cannot detect the juncture of the skilful mosaic, the spirit is apprised of disunion, simply by the failure to affect the spirit."[49] The writer must not sink to cohere. "The mark of genius is, that it has not only thoughts, but the copula that joins them is also a thought."[50]

Shortly before the first series of *Essays* was ready for the printer, Emerson vented in his journal his disgust at the apparent necessity of making concessions in this direction: "I have been writing with some pains essays on various matters as a sort of apology to my country for my apparent idleness. But the poor work has looked poorer daily, as I strove to end it. My genius seemed to quit me in such a mechanical work, a seeming wise—a cold exhibition of dead thoughts. When I write a letter to anyone whom I love, I have no lack of words or thoughts. I am wiser than myself and read my paper with the pleasure of one who receives a letter, but what I write to fill up the gaps of a chapter is hard and cold,

[45] *Jour.* II, 446.
[46] *Jour.* V, 79.
[47] *Jour.* IV, 336.
[48] *Natural History of Intellect: Walter Savage Landor*, 348.
[49] *Natural History of Intellect: Instinct and Inspiration*, 67.
[50] *Jour.* IX, 67-8.

is grammar and logic; there is no magic in it; I do not wish to see it again."[51] Two months later, on New Year's Day, 1841, a record in the journals shows that he has reached the conclusion that no transition is better than sham transition. "I begin the year by sending my little book of Essays to the press. What remains to be done to its imperfect chapters I will seek to do justly. I see no reason why we may not write with as much grandeur of spirit as we can serve or suffer. Let the page be filled with the character, not with the skill of the writer."[52]

Bacon's *prima philosophia*, being congruent both with the transcendental distinction between that which seems and that which is, and also with the relation between Each and All, has thus stretched a long hand over the centuries to affect the structure of a Yankee philosopher's essays. With their aid it has given him the high ambition to see all facts as shot through with the golden thread of spiritual unity. Whenever his vision has failed him, and he has been unable to follow the intricate course of the weaving, staunch Puritan honesty has prevented him from substituting an inferior pattern in his own attempts to copy the work of the Divine Designer.

In regard to the question of form in Emerson's essays Professor Firkins says (p. 238): "The pure or abstract essays are of looser fabric than the works strongly tinctured with concrete fact or practical import." What clearer indication could there be of the influence of his dualism on Emerson's method? In dealing with the material, a material form of organization can be quickly arrived at. In dealing with the spiritual a thousand-and-one difficulties, which we have suggested, hamper the author who seeks system. We can count on plan in an essay on Experience; we can hardly look for an obviously well-rounded essay on the Oversoul. And in the former of these essays, indeed, Emerson, before proceeding to his definitely arrived at conclusion, carefully reminds his reader of the subtopics which he has discussed. In the latter he can offer only an indefinitely merged series of "hints," which in this case certainly, because of the nature of the subject, have their principal connection in God.

In the midst of defeat of his desire to see identity in all kinds of variety, Emerson at times found consolation and even the hope of a certain kind of victory, though eternal truth rather than the mortal reader is the chief gainer thereby. By omitting the unmeant mechanical transition, he obtained, for one thing, the energizing effect of the pause, concerning which something was said in the section on Compression. These breaks may well be regarded as what Dr. Edward Emerson calls: "intervals for the electric spark to pass and thrill the reader."[53] But more important

[51] *Jour.* V, 469.
[52] *Jour.* V, 506.
[53] *Natural History of Intellect*, 439.

is the assurance which the Each and All theory gives him. By way of making amends for the stringent requirements it exacts from the philosopher or writer who is attempting to make a system, it gives aid and comfort to the person who has relinquished this idea because of his feeling of incapacity. For if, on the one hand, it insists that no organization can suffice which is not built upon the basis of a complete understanding of the relation of the Many to the One, it declares, on the other hand, that the Infinite is enclosed in every particle and system is after all unnecessary. Thus the same theory pulls in two different directions: it makes organization desirable but difficult; and it declares any such effort useless.

Two passages from the journals have already been given which express Emerson's views regarding the organization of the First Series of *Essays*. The first of these, it will be recalled, deals with the difficulties he found in writing suitable transitions; the second implies that honest incontinuity is better than a show of structural perfection. Between the dates of these two appears a paragraph which shows that he was at this time deriving some consolation from the Each and All theory, which had in this instance turned its encouraging cheek and offered so much, at least, of solace. After acknowledging his lack of system and his failure to come anywhere near completeness in his "Cabinet Cyclopædia" of "all the definitions at which the world had yet arrived," he says: "At last I discovered that my curve was a parabola whose arcs would never meet, and came to acquiesce in the perception that, although no diligence can rebuild the universe in a model by the best accumulation or disposition of details, yet does the world reproduce itself in miniature in every event that transpires, so that all the laws of nature may be read in the simplest fact. So that the truth-speaker may dismiss all solicitude as to the proportion and congruency of the aggregate of his thoughts, so long as he is a faithful reporter of particular impressions."[54]

Alas, poor reader! Emerson is much concerned that the writer shall be individual, but he assumes absolutely no personality in the writer's audience. He thinks only of the Universal Man with the Universal Mind, whose interest is not in the continuous reading of an hour,but in the ages long gathering of bits of spiritual information. Thus he finds another justification for his practice of writing inconsecutively in his journals the thoughts of the day or the moment, in the naturalness and hence the truth of such a method. Such thoughts, put together without pretence of system, are likely to have a noble unity all their own resulting from the divinity of their source. "But you say," he answers an imaginary critic, "that so moving and moved on thoughts and verses, gathered in different parts of a long life, you sail no straight line, but are perpetually distracted

[54] *Jour.* V, 326-7.

by new and counter currents, and go a little way north, then a little way northeast, then a little northwest, then a little north again, and so on.

"Be it so; is any motion different? The curve line is not a curve, but an infinite polygon. The voyage of the best ship is a zigzag line on a hundred tacks. This is only microscopic criticism. See the line from a sufficient distance, and it straightens itself to the average tendency. All these verses and thoughts were as spontaneous at some time to that man as any one was. Being so, they were not his own, but above him the voice of simple, necessary, aboriginal nature, and, coming from so narrow experience as one mortal, they must be strictly related, even the farthest ends of his life, and, seen at the perspective of a few ages, will appear harmonious and univocal."[55]

To the same effect he says, with reference, this time, to his inability to philosophize according to a system in the ordinary sense, "I cannot myself use that systematic form which is reckoned essential in treating the science of the mind. But if one can say so without arrogance, I might suggest that he who contents himself with dotting a fragmentary curve, recording only what facts he has observed, without attempting to arrange them within one outline, follows a system also,—a system as grand as any other, though he does not interfere with its vast curves by prematurely forcing them into a circle or ellipse, but only draws that arc which he clearly sees, or perhaps at a later observation a remote curve of the same orbit, and waits for a new opportunity, well assured that these observed arcs will consist with each other."[56]

Emerson's theories in regard to the organization of prose are exactly paralleled by his theories in regard to the structure of poetry; consequently discussion of the latter may well serve as summary of discussion of the former. Poetry is made from materials of similar size to those that make up prose; these require the same kind of arrangement. It, too, is composed of particles, the results of momentary inspiration, which it is the function of art to synthesize. "A poem should be a blade of Damascus steel, made up [of] a mass of knife-blades and nails, and parts every one of which has had its whole surface hammered and wrought before it was welded into the sword, to be wrought over anew."[57] "It is as lawful and as becoming for the poet to seize upon felicitous expressions and lay them up for use as for Michel Angelo to store his sketch-book with hands, arms, triglyphs, and capitals to enrich his future compositions. The wary artist in both kinds

[55] *Jour.* V, 224-5.
[56] *Natural History of Intellect: Powers and Laws of Thought*, 11-2.
[57] *Jour.* IV, 278.

will tear down the scaffolding when the work is finished, and himself supply no clue to the curiosity that would know how he did the wonder."[58]

Not only perfect fusion, but unity of design, thought, and tone are necessary in poetry as much as in prose. Of his friend Ellery Channing's verse, Emerson says: "His poetry is like the artless warbling of a vireo, which whistles prettily all day and all summer in the elm, but never rounds a tune, nor can increase the value of melody by the power of composition and cuneiform determination. He must have construction also."[59] Unity of thought and tone are almost inseparable. "The authentic mark of a new poem" is "the uncontrollable interior impulse . . . which is unanalysable, and makes the merit of an ode of Collins, or Gray, or Wordsworth, or Herbert, or Byron,—and which is felt in the pervading tone, rather than in brilliant parts or lines; as if the sound of a bell, or a certain cadence expressed in a low whistle or booming, or humming, to which the poet first timed his step, as he looked at the sunset, or thought, was the incipient form of the piece, and was regnant through the whole."[60] "One genial thought is the source of every true poem. I have heard that a unity of this kind pervades Beethoven's great pieces in music. And why, but because tone gives unity?"[61]

And as Emerson recognized his infirmity in matters of form so far as prose was concerned, so he acknowledged his weakness in the same regard poetically. "It is much," he says, "to write sentences; it is more to add method and write out the spirit of your life symmetrically. But to arrange general reflections in their natural order, so that I shall have one homogeneous piece,—a Lycidas, an Allegro, a Hamlet, a Midsummer Night's Dream,—this continuity is for the great. The wonderful men are wonderful hereby. Such concentration of experiences is in every good work, which, though successive in the mind of the master, were primarily combined in his piece. But what we want is consecutiveness. 'Tis with us a flash of light, then a long darkness, then a flash again. Ah! could we turn these fugitive sparkles into an astronomy of Copernican worlds."[62] To the same effect he writes in his journal, again conscious of his failure in larger units, and of his success, brilliant but fragmentary, in the smaller: "I am a bard least of bards. I cannot, like them, make lofty arguments in stately, continuous verse, constraining the rocks, trees, animals, and the periodic stars to say my thoughts,—for that is the gift of great poets; but I am a bard because I stand near them, and apprehend all they utter, and with pure joy hear that which I also would say, and, moreover, I speak inter-

[58] *Jour.* III, 396.
[59] *Jour.* IX, 54.
[60] *Jour.* X, 267.
[61] *Jour.* X, 278.
[62] *Natural History of Intellect: Powers and Laws of Thought*, 52-3.

ruptedly words and half stanzas which have the like scope and aim:—What I cannot declare, yet cannot all withhold."[63]

Emerson found some comfort in partial achievement, and he gained more, as he did in the like situation in the field of prose, through the Each and All theory. The wish to see identity in variety results in making many of his poems, like many paragraphs in the essays, consist of an indefinite number of examples or symbols pointing at some ideal principle. Such poems, as Professor Firkins has pointed out, are often ineffective as well as structurally indefensible. But the same theory which is responsible for them is also to be credited with the production of such poems as *May-Day*, and with the fact that literature has been enriched by many lines of Emerson's authorship, whatever may be said of complete poems. "The poem," in Emerson's opinion, "is made up of lines each of which filled the sky of the poet in its turn,"[64] each of which, in other words, momentarily epitomized eternity for him. The great poet, Emerson believes, combines such lines and puts them under the sway of masterly method and a centralizing conception. The minor poet can but arrange them successively and hope, as Emerson hoped in regard to his prose, either that the infinitely extensible fragments will each in its turn represent infinity, or that a kind of unity will grow out of their uniform divinity of origin. *May-Day* stands as the result of a deliberate carrying out of the latter hope; it is the mere addition of a large number of springtime images, written from day to day in the journals. Many would wish these images devoted to a lofty unifying purpose, but no one would deny their high poetic merit or wish them destroyed because they are not so utilized. And for their preservation in print, the Each and All theory deserves the credit.

Professor Firkins defends Emerson's poetry on the ground that the most poetic thing about poetry is its particular images. "If a man utter a phrase like 'burly, dozing humble-bee,' does it really matter so much whether he can repeat or sustain or enforce it in the succeeding lines or stanzas?"[65] And though Emerson himself demanded structure as the necessary qualification of supreme verse, he tested poetry in this way. He tells us of a conversation with Tennyson regarding that always huge and now dusty epic, *Festus*. "When *Festus* was spoken of, I said that a poem must be made up of little poems, but that in *Festus* were no single good lines; you could not quote one line. Tennyson quoted—

> 'There came a hand between the sun and us,
> And its five fingers made five nights in air.'"[66]

Tennyson had picked out for him the most Tennysonian lines in *Festus*!

[63] *Jour.* IX, 472.
[64] *Jour.* X, 464.
[65] *Ralph Waldo Emerson*, 295.
[66] *Jour.* VII, 445.

In poetry, as in prose, Emerson found value in the mere collection of meteoric particles, since the ability to create astronomic systems or even constellations was denied him. Better this, he thought, than to synthesize an artificial cosmogony through a mixture of star chips with base earth.

One more influence of dualism on Emerson's organization is worth mention, though this is evident only in practice and not definitely proclaimed in theory. Many of the essays derive their structure from a balancing of the material with the ideal. The essay on *Fate* in *Conduct of Life*, for instance, after devoting most of its contents to pointing out the varied strength of terrible necessity, suddenly contrasts its force with that of Intellect, which "annuls Fate." The chapter on *Literature* in *English Traits*, after praising English writers for their accurate embodiment of the apparent, alternately blames and praises English literature because of its modern deficiency in Platonists and its former glory. The essays in *Representative Men* are built on the same scheme. We marvel at Napoleon's possession of common sense and executive power, and then shudder at his immorality. Montaigne's scepticism and solidity are admirable, but scepticism can never take the place of faith. Shakspeare has commanding merits as a user of the symbol, but how much greater he would have been if he had only lived ideally!

Dualism is Emerson's guide and comforter in matters of system, whether they be philosophical or literary. It gives him from time to time visionary glimpses of the Promised Land; and though he is never permitted to enter into it, he can group these momentary impressions in such a way as to enjoy some of its blessings if only in vague and irregular anticipations. The length and breadth of Canaan he can never know; but he can climb Pisgah often enough to become familiar with the silver of its streams, the green of its distant valleys, and the misty blue of its mountain peaks.

THE GROWTH OF EMERSON'S THEORIES OF STYLE

Emerson's pages often bristle with quotations which, though they tend in the same direction as his own thought, suggest rather the sedulous Burton than the inspired sage. But as parallels and seeming sources of an Emersonian doctrine increase in number, the likelihood grows that, after all, he has a native right to the doctrine in question. For it was his habit to read literature not with an eye to the novelties which others might have to offer, but looking rather for support and illustration of his original beliefs. In an inquiry concerning the germination and growth of his theories of style, therefore, it is, strictly speaking, not so much sources that are to be sought, as the encouragements of predisposition.

Our examination of influences falls into two parts: (1) the causes and development of Emerson's high regard for the symbol; (2) the causes leading to the squaring of this regard with admiration of a simple, idiomatic, compressed and repressed—and above all *living* style.

The difference in Emerson's mature attitude toward the symbol from his earlier attitude, and from that of most writers, is that he considers the figure as having a spiritual life and reality of its own, and does not regard it as merely an imaginative identification of one thing with another for purely literary, artistic purposes. He sees between the mental and the physical not an accidental but a divinely purposed analogical import, which results from his belief that nature and experience—all material things—are the language of spirit. As a consequence of these conceptions, he desires in the symbol an intimate blending of the actual and the ideal, of spiritual truth with corporeal accuracy.

This attitude is the result of ideal dualism. In seeing the causes of Emerson's high esteem of the symbol, then, it is necessary to look first for the origins of his dualism, and to notice also, as we proceed, the influences which were exerted upon it.

Emerson was a Platonist not by books, but by birth. "As a boy he had rejoiced in Berkeley's idealism, and the poems of the holy Herbert."[1] His mind was naturally enamored, not only, as he said, of moral perfection, but of differences between the physical and the divine. At the age of 21, at least five years before Coleridge had acquainted him with the distinction between the Understanding and the Reason, he estimates his fitness for the ministry on grounds which show that he draws the distinction though he knows nothing of Kant and his nomenclature. "I have, or had, a strong imagination, and consequently a keen relish for the beauties of poetry. . . . My reasoning faculty is proportionably weak, nor can I ever

[1] *English Traits*, 324.

hope to write a Butler's Analogy or an Essay of Hume. Nor is it strange that with this confession I should choose theology, which is from everlasting to everlasting 'debateable ground.' For, the highest species of reasoning upon divine subjects is rather the fruit of a sort of moral imagination, than of the 'Reasoning Machines,' such as Locke and Clarke and David Hume. Dr. Channing's Dudleian Lecture is the model of what I mean, and the faculty which produced this is akin to the higher flights of the fancy. I may add that the preaching most in vogue at the present day depends chiefly on imagination for its success, and asks those accomplishments which I believe are most within my grasp."[2]

The mind of religious and imaginative cast, with a tendency to draw a line between the things of sense and logic and those of the more lofty intuititions, will soon see the literary value and importance of the symbol. Several records in the journals written during Emerson's college years make plain his recognition of its worth. In poetry he sees an elevated expression of the passions revealed especially in their "tendency . . . to clothe fanciful views of objects in beautiful language;" a tendency which "seems to consist in the pleasure of finding out a connection between a material image and a moral sentiment." The relation between science and poetry is that "Science penetrates the sky, ... and Poetry grasps at its striking phenomena and combines them with the moral sentiment which they naturally suggest."[3] And this relation, Emerson notes, the philosopher takes advantage of to make himself understood. He "who speculates on mind or character" cannot hope to be intelligible "until he borrows the emphatic imagery of sense;"[4] he must possess the "philosophic imagination," for "moral reflections are vague and fugitive, whereas the most vulgar mind can readily retain a striking image from the material world."[5]

Emerson needed no outside influence to make him perceive the value of figures of speech to poet, philosopher, and preacher as the means by which they might embody abstractions. No contemporary, but a long line of spiritual-minded forebears had planted the seed of idealism which Berkeley and Channing had caused to sprout. An external force, however, was needed to enable him to realize fully the consequences of the relation between the moral and mental on the one hand, and the physical on the other. He saw a philosophical and religious division between these, and a stylistic connection; but he did not put the two conceptions together. He saw only an artistic correspondence between high thoughts and the objects of nature. At the age of 16, it is true, he was pleased by Chateaubriand's

[2] *Jour.* I, 361.
[3] *Jour.* I, 105.
[4] *Jour.* I, 348.
[5] *Jour.* I, 323.

saying that "the universe is the imagination of the deity made manifest;"[6] but only the fact that he repeats this quotation sixteen years later[7] suggests that the thought of this kind of kinship between God and nature must have lingered in his mind. He certainly made no immediate application of it to language. His attitude toward figures of speech is rather that of his contemporaries toward the floridity so common in the sermons and orations of the day. The gaudy or elegant tropes of Everett or of Buckminster stimulated his esthetic or dramatic rather than his spiritual sensibilities.

New light came from a little book, published in 1826, *Observations on the Growth of the Mind.* It was an unpretentious primer of Swedenborgianism by Sampson Reed, a Boston druggist; clear in style but undistinguished except for a quiet sincerity of tone, sometimes heightened to a poetic warmth. It bears in thought an obvious relationship to Emerson's first *Nature*, but it lacks the glow and fervor of that essay. It made a profound impression upon Emerson, "a revelation, such is the wealth and such is the novelty of the truth unfolded in it."[8] This high opinion of the book continued. In October, 1826, a month after the entry in the journals just cited, he writes to his aunt asking her why she does not like the book. "The Sabbath after it came out, Dr. Channing delivered a discourse obviously founded upon it."[9] In 1834 Emerson recommended the book to James Freeman Clarke[10] and to Carlyle, and in fact sent Carlyle a copy.[11] In 1836, he writes to his brother William that the contents of his book *Nature* "will not exceed in bulk Sampson Reed's 'Growth of the Mind.' "[12]

"Has any modern hand touched the harp of great nature so rarely? Has any looked so shrewdly into the subtile and concealed connection of man and nature, of earth and heaven?"[13] These questions, in which Emerson communicated his enthusiasm about the book to his Aunt Mary, suggest the kind of new truths he found in it. It enabled him to link the earthly and the heavenly in addition to discriminating between them; and thus furnished him with a spiritual explanation and justification of the use of the symbol. Three sentences from *The Growth of the Mind* will make plain the identity of its ideas on this point with those that Emerson later expressed. "By poetry is meant all those illustrations of truth by natural imagery, which spring from the fact that this world is the mirror

[6] *Jour.* I, 13-4.
[7] *Jour.* IV, 76.
[8] *Jour.* II, 116-7.
[9] *Jour.* II, 124.
[10] *Jour.* II, 116 Note.
[11] *C. E. Corr.* I, 16.
[12] *Memoir* I, 259.
[13] *Jour.* II, 124.

of him who made it." "Finding a resting-place in every created object," imagination "will enter into it to explore its hidden treasures, the relation in which it stands to mind, and reveal the love it bears to its Creator." "When there shall be a religion which shall see God in everything at all times; and the natural sciences, not less than nature itself, shall be regarded in connection with him; the fire of poetry will begin to be kindled in its immortal part, and will burn without consuming." These conceptions are exactly consonant with Emerson's beliefs that nature is God's language as well as man's; that every part of nature is divinely significant; and that science is valuable only because of its spiritual affinities.

Thus Swedenborg, through Sampson Reed, changed Emerson's attitude toward the symbol. Evidence of this is furnished by the contrast between the ideas just expressed and those that Emerson himself set down a few months before he had read *The Growth of the Mind*. Wordsworth's poetry is the subject of discussion. Emerson compares his philosophy of poetry with "the undisciplined enterprizes of intellect in the middle age"; the attempts to extort the secrets of nature by alchemy, for instance. He continues in a fashion Dr. Johnson would have approved: "Not otherwise this modern poet . . . has discarded that modesty under whose influence all his great precursors have resorted to external nature sparingly for illustration and ornament, and have forborne to tamper with the secret and metaphysical nature of what they borrowed. . . He can't be satisfied with feeling the general beauty of a moonlight evening, or of a rose. He would pick them to pieces and pounce on the pleasurable element he is sure is in them, like the little boy who cut open his drum to see what made the noise. The worthy gentleman gloats over a bulrush, moralizes on the irregularity of one of its fibres, and suspects a connection between an excrescence of the plant and its own immortality. Is it not much more comformable to that golden middle line in which all that is good and wise of life lies, to let what Heaven made small and casual remain the objects of a notice small and casual, and husband our admiration for images of grandeur in matters or in mind?"[14]

This neo-classical view is totally at variance with that of Sampson Reed and that of the transcendental Emerson. External nature is to them the source of all that is holy in poetry. In their opinion, every object in nature, no matter how small, deserves attention; it is the duty of imagination to "enter into it to explore its hidden treasures," as Reed expresses it. What a change Reed has wrought is evident in what, five years later, Emerson said regarding Wordsworth's *Dion*: "Are not things eternal exactly in the proportion in which they enter inward into nature; eternal according to their *in*ness?"[15]

[14] *Jour.* II, 105-110.
[15] *Jour.* II, 429.

Early in 1827, the next year after the publication of *The Growth of the Mind*, Emerson uses for the first time the term *Transcendentalism*, calling it one of the "peculiarities of the present age." He defines it thus: "Metaphysics and Ethics look inwards—and France produces Mad. de Staël; England, Wordsworth; America, Sampson Reed; as well as Germany, Swedenborg."[16] The omission of Kant in such a list is curious, especially as Emerson had read Madame de Staël's *Germany* and had made extracts from it in November 1826.[17] Later, in the lecture called *The Transcendentalist*[18] Emersôn gave Kant full credit as the father of transcendentalism and the popularizer of the term. There is no doubt, however, that at this time and later Emerson thought of the transcendental symbol as primarily exemplified by Swedenborg. "I am glad you like Sampson Reed," he writes to Carlyle in 1834. "Swedenborgianism . . . has many points of attraction for you . . . for" the Swedenborgians "esteem, in common with all the Trismegisti, the Natural World as strictly the symbol or exponent of the spiritual."[19] In 1842, the journals contain this record: "I began to write of Poetry and was driven at once to think of Swedenborg as the person who, of all the men in the recent ages, stands eminently for the translator of Nature into thought."[20] And in the lecture on *Poetry and Imagination*[21] occurs a passage which is its own best commentary on the criticism previously quoted regarding Wordsworth's tendency to go to Nature extravagantly for illustration of thought: "I count the genius of Swedenborg and Wordsworth as the agents of a reform in philosophy, the bringing poetry back to Nature,—to the marrying of Nature and mind, undoing the old divorce in which poetry had been famished and false, and Nature had been suspected and pagan." Yet until Emerson read Sampson Reed, nature had been for him suspected and pagan, especially in the poems of Wordsworth.

Some contribution to Emerson's conception of the symbol came from Jeffrey's Edinburgh[22] review of Alison on *Taste*. Emerson noted in 1823 that the review "gives an excellent condensed view"[23] of Alison's theory. Jeffrey and Alison were far from being transcendentalists, but they did believe that beauty in poetry is produced by associating ideas with the objects of outer nature. That Emerson took one step farther and converted this to transcendental purposes is shown by a paragraph in the journals of 1832. "A strange poem is Zoroastrism. It is a system as separate and

[16] *Jour.* II, 164.
[17] *Jour.* II, 129.
[18] *Nature, etc.*, 339-40.
[19] *C. E. Corr.* I, 32.
[20] *Jour.* VI, 185.
[21] *Letters, etc.*, 66.
[22] V, iii.
[23] *Jour.* I, 293.

harmonious and sublime as Swedenborgianism—congruent. One would be glad to behold the truth which they all shadow forth. For it cannot but be truth that they typify and symbolize. . . One sees in this, and in them all, the element of poetry according to Jeffrey's true theory, the effect produced by making every thing outward only a sign of something inward: Plato's *forms or ideas* which seem almost tantamount to the Ferouers of Zoroaster."[24]

More direct seems to have been Jeffrey's offering to another aspect of Emerson's theory of language. Emerson says in his chapter on *Language* in *Nature:* "Every word which is used to express a moral or intellectual fact, if traced to its root, is found to be borrowed from some material appearance." Jeffrey says in his review of Alison: "Almost all the words by which the affections of the mind are expressed, seem to have been borrowed originally from the qualities of matter." Of course, Emerson may have arrived at the idea independently, or he may have got it from other sources: Plato's *Cratylus*, as Professor Harrison declares,[25] or the chapter on the *Symbol* in *Sartor Resartus*. On the other hand the verbal parallelism of the two sentences quoted may be significant.

There are many indications that interest in the symbol is an inevitable outcome of transcendentalism. We have just mentioned the chapter in *Sartor*. Another example is Alcott's practical application of the symbol to young children's education, commented on with approval by Emerson.[26] But so far as Emerson is concerned, these are not to be regarded as influential, except insofar as the encouragement comes from the agreement of others in his already formed ideas. For both these examples are of later date[27] than passages in the journals which show unmistakably his belief in the correlation of nature and language. In 1831, perhaps before he had read Carlyle at all, except for the translation of *Wilhelm Meister*,[28] he expressed his desire to "get the abstract sense of which mountains, sunshine, thunders, night, birds and flowers are the sublime alphabet," and to "translate the fair and magnificent symbols into their own sentiments."[29]

Four years later he was much interested in a book by a minor French philosopher, Oegger. Many pages in the journals for 1835, the year before the publication of *Nature*, contain quotations from Oegger's *The True Messiah, or the Old and New Testaments examined according to the Principles of the Language of Nature*. The translator was Miss Elizabeth Peabody, who helped to teach Alcott's school in which the symbol formed the starting-

[24] *Jour.* II, 473-4.

[25] *The Teachers of Emerson*, 35.

[26] *Jour.* III, 509.

[27] 1835 and 1832-3 respectively.

[28] Carlyle makes his first appearance in the *Journals* (II, 515) October 1, 1832, as "my Germanick new-light writer, whoever he be."

[29] *Jour.* II, 385.

point of instruction. "Why the world exists, and that it exists for a language or medium whereby God may speak to man, this is his query, this his answer," is Emerson's summary of the book.[30] The chapter on *Language* in *Nature* parallels Oegger's contention that the voice of Nature is the voice of God, and includes a direct quotation from him: "Material objects are necessarily kinds of *scoriae* of the substantial thoughts of the Creator."[31] To Oegger Emerson is indebted, not only for this quotation, but also for his psychological argument in the chapter to the effect that symbols are the constant mental accompaniment of high thought. "I must scribble on," he writes, "if it were only to say in confirmation of Oegger's doctrine that I believe I never take a step in thought when engaged in conversation without some material symbol of my proposition figuring itself incipiently at the same time."[32] But so far as Oegger's principal thesis is concerned, Emerson had, as we have seen, read, approved, and adopted a like theory as expressed in Sampson Reed's little volume.

More difficult to follow with definiteness is the direct influence of Plato on Emerson's conception of the symbol. Swedenborg draws on Plato, of course, as do all the other mystics, and we shall see soon an important Platonic influence through the medium of Coleridge. But direct and specific references are not frequent, and it seems likely that in these cases Emerson is adducing a parallel rather than indicating a source. Of this character appears to be his connection of the figure of the cave in the *Republic* with his own attitude toward symbols, shown in the quotation already given concerning Zoroaster and Jeffrey; and the same kind of relationship is likely to account for his mention, in the essay on Plato in *Representative Men*, of the analogy of the divided line. Though there are many points of similarity between Emerson's ideas and Plato's, and many cases of direct borrowing, since Emerson took what he wished where he found it, it seems likely that with regard to the symbol, at least, Plato's dualism had on Emerson's conceptions only a general influence.

From Wordsworth Emerson gained assistance in regarding the yellow primrose as something more than a primrose, though Sampson Reed had to intervene before he was converted from an early hostile attitude. From Wordsworth, also, his interest in idiomatic language may have received stimulation. Both Wordsworth's *Preface* and Plato's *Republic* may have something to do with his belief that the simple life, close to Nature, is best for the poet. But for this his Aunt Mary probably deserves as much credit. For in a letter dated 1823 he says that his aunt "was anxious that her nephew might hold high and reverential notions regarding it [nature], as the temple where God and the mind are to be studied and adored, and where

[30] *Jour.* III, 525.
[31] *Jour.* III, 513.
[32] *Jour.* III, 527.

the fiery souls can begin a premature communication with the other world."[33] His personal experience also led in the same direction. It caused him to believe in his aunt's prescription of nature as a source of inspiration, for he writes that his brain had been supplied "with several bright fragments of thought" and that he had come to believe that "mind as well as body respired more freely here."[34] Later vacation trips in the wilds had an even stronger effect, for at these times he went into the woods impressed by a theoretical conviction of the close correlation of God and nature. Finally, his life in Concord, as has been shown in the chapter on the *Symbol*, led to a veritable ecstasy of communion with nature, with the effect of an emotional heightening of his style.

Influence of a general kind came from two other quarters: Madame de Staël and Coleridge. Madame de Staël's *Germany* gave him his first literary knowledge of the German philosophers, including Kant; and her whole attitude is such as to cause Emerson to rank her, as we have seen, as the French exemplar of transcendentalism, and to place her among his favorite authors.

Coleridge he read with enthusiasm three years later, in 1829. From him he gained, if not the important conception, at least the important nomenclature, involved in Kant's distinction between the Reason and the Understanding. The interaction of this distinction with his theory of style has been evident many times in these pages, for the Reason, being the ideal part of the mind, is the symbol-perceiving faculty.

Professor Harrison in *The Teachers of Emerson* offers nothing more important than the specific evidence that Coleridge's *Friend* is probably responsible in some degree for Emerson's attitude toward science. Emerson regarded natural laws as parallel with spiritual, and it is Professor Harrison's contention that Coleridge, who brings to his aid Plato and Bacon, had helped to make this Emerson's opinion. Of course, so far as Bacon is concerned, Emerson may have gained the notion independently of Coleridge, for youthful enthusiasm gave him a thorough acquaintance with Bacon, and he may then have noted the Baconian examples of analogies between physical and mental or moral laws, which appear in the criticism on Bacon in *English Traits*, in connection with discussion of the *prima philosophia*. Whatever Coleridge's influence may have been in this direction, it is certain that De Gérando's *Histoire Comparée des Systèmes*, which Emerson studied in 1830, reminded him of his early reading in Bacon, "leads me in the outset back to Bacon,"[35] as he says. And it is equally sure that the first mention of the *prima philosophia*, of which these analogies are examples, occurs in the notes which he took on De Gérando's compila-

[33] *Memoirs:* I, 97.
[34] Ibid.
[35] *Jour.* II, 330.

tion. That Sampson Reed may also be partly responsible for Emerson's poetical point of view toward science we have already seen in Reed's wish that "the natural sciences, as well as Nature itself, should be seen in connection with" God, valued for their spiritual intimations. In any case, it was in the latter part of 1830, after he had read both *The Friend* and the *Histoire Comparée*, when Emerson, being "more and more impressed," as the editors of the Journals say, "that Nature spoke by parables, . . . began to read books on science with keen interest."[36] The strength of the interest appears in the fact that his earliest lectures and his latest involved natural history, both of the outer world and of the intellect.

Associated with this interest in science and partly derived from the same sources in Coleridge, Bacon, and De Gérando, is the Each and All theory, which is concerned with the underlying cause of the correlation between spiritual and material laws. According to both Coleridge and Bacon this is a "supersensual essence," which, Coleridge says, Plato has shown to be the "ground of the coincidence between reason and experience; or between the laws of matter and the ideas of the pure intellect."[37] Coleridge may also have suggested to Emerson that the laws of this spiritual essence were equivalent to the laws of Bacon's First Philosophy, since, as Professor Harrison has pointed out, Coleridge contrasts Plato's philosophic system with Bacon's scientific theory.[38] It is more likely, however, that De Gérando is responsible, for reasons stated in the preceding paragraph. It is interesting to note that having quoted Bacon's definition of the *prima philosophia* from De Gérando, Emerson comments: "By this I understand that generalization which gives the elevation to all the writings of Burke, of De Staël, and now of Sampson Reed."[39]

The principle controlling the relation between matter and spirit, and the laws of each, makes it possible—so Plato, Bacon, Coleridge, Emerson, and De Gérando believe—to classify spiritually all material facts, to see identity in variety. Emerson is fond of the phrase *il più nell'uno*, " 'the many in one,' or multitude in unity, intimating that what is truly beautiful seems related to all nature."[40] He defines the purpose of Art as the showing of this relation. But the Each and All theory not only provides a means of classification; it makes possible a magnificent generalization from single and unconnected instances. And thus Emerson is equally interested in showing that "All is in Each," that spiritual completeness is inherent in every material particle. One sentence from the essay on Swedenborg in *Representative Men* (pp. 113-4) gives so many parallels of this idea that the

[36] *Jour.* II, 365 Note.

[37] *The Friend* II, quoted by J. S. Harrison: *The Teachers of Emerson*, 44.

[38] *The Teachers of Emerson*, 22-3.

[39] *Jour.* II, 331.

[40] *Natural History of Intellect: Michael Angelo*, 218.

likelihood of any one or perhaps even all of them together being a source is thereby diminished. "The ancient doctrine of Hippocrates, that the brain is a gland; and of Leucippus, that the atom may be known by the mass; or, in Plato, the macrocosm by the microcosm; and, in the verses of Lucretius,— . . .

> The principle of all things, entrails made
> Of smallest entrails; bone, of smallest bone;
> Blood, of small sanguine drops reduced to one;
> Gold, of small grains; earth, of small sands compacted;
> Small drops to water, sparks to fire contracted:

and which Malpighi had summed in his maxim that 'nature exists entire in leasts,'—is a favorite thought of Swedenborg."

These philosophic and scientific ideas are worked into Emerson's theory of style as a result of the religious revolt against dogmatism and fossilized divinity which marked the years from 1820 to 1840 in New England. Though Emerson as a youth believed his vocation to be rightly the Christian Church, as early as 1824 he writes an imaginary letter to Plato in which he expresses his belief that the Bible, though inspired, is not inspiration itself. "I confess it has not for me the same exclusive and extraordinary claims it has for many. I hold Reason to be a prior Revelation and that they do not contradict each other."[41] Sampson Reed strengthens his independence by assuring him that the divine message may be read in every part of nature at all times. And it is notable that in September 1826, just after he had read *The Growth of the Mind* for the first time, he writes thus to his aunt: "It is one of the feelings of modern philosophy that it is wrong to regard ourselves so much in an historical light as we do,—putting Time between God and us,—and that it were fitter to regard every moment of the existence of the universe as a new creation, and all as a revelation proceeding each moment from the Divinity to the mind of the observer."[42] This belief grew stronger when Emerson had given up the ministry, and was confirmed through other influences contributing to self-reliance already detailed in the chapter on *Method*. The result of the application of this conviction to writing is to make the journals more and more the record of intense moments. In each of these momentary impressions, Emerson grew to believe that divine unity was contained. Thus the philosophical and scientific aspects of the Each and All theory merged with the religious belief that God revealed himself at all times to every man in every part of nature and experience. The manifold effects of this on Emerson's theories of diction and method have been sufficiently touched on elsewhere in these pages.

[41] *Jour.* I, 386.
[42] *Memoir* I, 159-60.

Swedenborg, though in large measure responsible for bringing this theory in both scientific and religious aspects to Emerson's attention, did not himself apply it flexibly. He regarded each part of nature as fixedly meaning just one spiritual truth. Emerson, on the other hand, regarded every part as interchangeable with every other, because all parts share the divine unity; and thus he considered each part as open to an endless variety of symbolic interpretations. Hence the Each and All theory becomes of primary importance in connection with Emerson's devotion to a living, breathing, modern style, which is at the same time spiritual because symbolic. If God reveals himself in every moment in every part of Nature, the writer's object must be to distill the spiritual life of any particular moment in a unique symbol. But if the same object in another equally inspired moment suggests other divine truth, the process of capturing the moment alive may be repeated with just as important results.

The religious and literary independence of attitude which characterizes transcendentalism thus makes it possible for the writer to utilize any object in nature, no matter how small, common, and unregarded, and to find in it spiritual significance. And it is in this way that the Each and All theory justifies use of the ordinary objects of life, experience, and nature, and makes desirable a style which is both simple and alive. It comes into alignment, in ways examined in detail elsewhere, with admiration of the style which is idiomatic, compact, and suggestively moderate.

Emerson's devotion to these qualities, however, is not altogether dependent on the doctrine of Each and All, but is at the same time consequent upon the general encouragement to individualism which transcendentalism offers. Transcendentalism asserts that every man, through his personal share of inspiration, hears God's voice. It gives him, therefore, self-reliance to deliver the divine message in a manner obviously his and no one else's. It causes the writer to throw away allegiance to rhetorical textbooks and conventionalized judgments of literature. Emerson speaks of "that barren season of discipline which young men spend with the Aikens and Ketts and Drakes and Blairs; acquiring the false doctrine that there is something arbitrary or conventional in letters, something else in style than the transparent medium through which we should see new and good thoughts."[43] Accordingly, transcendental individualism makes for distinctiveness and may make for distinction in style. It produces a style which tries to come close to the writer's own mind, and aims at phonographic reproduction of its ecstacy, its violence, its calmness, its humor, its seriousness, its holiness, or whatever its mood may be. Carlyle's style, for instance, defies and disregards conventions and gives us the tumultuous, dyspeptic, dead in earnest, irrepressible roughrider himself. It is a living

[43] *Memoir* I, 235.

style, exactly the kind which Carlyle describes in his review of Richter.[44] It is Carlyle's conviction "that the outward style is to be judged of by the inward qualities of the spirit which it is employed to body forth; that without prejudice to critical propriety well understood, the former may vary into many shapes as the latter varies; that, in short, the grand point for a writer is not to be of this or that external make and fashion, but, in every fashion, to be genuine, vigorous, alive—alive with his whole being, consciously, and for beneficient results."

Emerson, too, sought individual expression, but in his case the uniqueness desired is the result of a careful attempt to arrive at unusual symbols, to use the commonest objects in uncommon ways, to extract, even to extort from the familiar a new indication of the underlying identity. And he, too, wishes life, but in his case vitality grows out of his effort to make the spiritual thought palpitant with the nervous action, the breathing, the pulsation of the material thing. He wishes to transfer to the realm of the ideal imagination the corporeal definiteness and constant stirring vitality of nature. "Cut these words and they would bleed; they are vascular and alive," he says of Montaigne's style; and the same could be said of much of his own writing.

Montaigne, indeed, has a style compounded of the elements which Emerson most admired. Delight in Montaigne's expression appears in the essay in *Representative Men*, where Emerson notes its closeness to life and experience as revealed in its conversational and positive character. But to Montaigne he owes more than stylistic example; he found in his essays also direct exposition of stylistic qualities. In 1834 he writes in his journal: "Glad to read in my old gossip Montaigne some robust rules of rhetoric: I will have a chapter thereon in my book."[45] And he gives us a reference which enables us to discover the rules in question.

Montaigne, in that essay which perhaps more than any other of his should be called *Upon Everything in General*, but which bears a title that gives just as much excuse for rambling, *Upon Some Verses of Virgil*, happens at the moment to be speaking of the language of Virgil and Lucretius, and is led from that to set forth his stylistic opinions. He speaks first of his liking for an expression which is sinewy, compressed, and continuously aphoristic: "Their language is downright, and full of natural and continued vigor; they are all epigram; not only the tail, but the head, body, and feet. There is nothing forced, nothing languishing, but everything keeps the same pace:—

'Contextus totus virilis est; non sunt circa flosculos occupati.'

'Tis not a soft eloquence, and without offence only; 'tis nervous and solid, that does not so much please, as it fills and ravishes the greatest minds."

[44] *Works of Thomas Carlyle, Centenary Edition, Critical and Miscellaneous Essays* v. i.: *Jean Paul Friedrich Richter*, 19.

[45] *Jour.* III, 272.

This constantly extraordinary style, Montaigne then says, is the result of deep and vigorous thinking, and is, because of its origin, effective connotatively as well as denotatively. "This painting is not so much carried on by dexterity of hand as by having the object more vividly imprinted in the soul. Gallus speaks simply because he conceives simply: Horace sees farther and more clearly into things; his mind breaks into and rummages all the magazine of words and figures wherewith to express himself, and he must have them more than ordinary, because his conception is so. Plutarch says that he sees the Latin tongue by the things: 'tis here the same: the sense illuminates and produces the words, not words of air, but of flesh and bone; they signify more than they say."

Finally, Montaigne makes the point that writers of this kind attain their end in style not by neologisms but by an original use of everyday materials. "The handling and utterance of fine wits is that which sets off language; not so much by innovating it, as by putting it to more vigorous and varied services, and by straining, bending, and adapting it to them. They do not create words, but they enrich their own, and give them weight and signification by the uses they put them to, and teach them unwonted motions . . . There is stuff enough in our language, but there is a defect in cutting out; for there is nothing that might not be made out of our terms of hunting and war, which is a fruitful soil to borrow from; and forms of speaking, like herbs, improve and grow stronger by being transplanted."

A tight, sustained, nervous style, suggestive because vital, a style which makes deliberately unusual use of the common and the idiomatic—there could hardly be a better statement of Emerson's stylistic aims. The early date of the journal reference to these "rules of rhetoric," 1834, suggests that Montaigne thus became Emerson's preceptor not only—as has been said in the chapter on *Method*—in the matter of self-reliant writing on the basis of personal experience, but also with regard to specific qualities of diction.

Before this time Emerson favored simplicity in word and illustration, as has been shown elsewhere; and in college, many years previous, E. T. Channing, his composition teacher, had counseled an unpretentious, compressed, precise style.[46] But there is nothing here that suggests the athletic intensity which came to characterize his style in later years. This, indeed, did not make its appearance consistently till late in the thirties. *Nature*, 1836, has a different kind of intensity in places— the rapture of ecstasy; but it is not tinglingly vibrant like many of the subsequent essays. The addition of this electricity to Emerson's stylistic resources seems to have come about as the result of the combination of Montaigne's influence and that of the Each and All theory in support of the specific stylistic qualities mentioned, with the aid by example of much reading in sixteenth and seventeenth century English literature.

[46] A. P. Peabody: *Harvard Reminiscences.*

In 1836 Emerson had not definitely applied the Each and All theory to art, but in the next two years he did so, as is evident in *Michael Angelo*[47] and *The American Scholar*,[48] both of 1838. In the former the relation is set forth generally; in the latter are emphasized the importance of experience for the writer's equipment, and the desirability of that general democratization which has changed and enriched the subject-matter of literature by making possible symbolic use of the humblest objects. By 1838, Emerson is fully conscious of the definite stylistic qualities he favored. This is evident in his comments made in that year on the English literature of the sixteenth and seventeenth centuries. Here appears another probable influence by example. He read widely and sympathetically in the books of these centuries, for many of the writers are Platonists, and he regarded the literature of the period as prevailingly dualistic in character.[49] He is one of many nineteenth century essayists whose minds were steeped in the writings of the seventeenth century, and who accordingly went and wrote likewise. He finds in these writings "greater freedom, less affectation, greater emphasis, bolder figure and homelier idiom" than in modern books.[50] Thus his favorite stylistic qualities have a kind of filial retrospect, to borrow his phrase, to Montaigne, the Each and All theory, and Elizabethan and Jacobean literature.

Summary of the elements in the growth of Emerson's theories of style may well be accompanied by some account of the development of the style itself. Until 1830 or later, he wrote a sedately intellectual, ministerial style which had the requisite wholeness of good tissue that Arnold failed to discover in his later work. It has all the continuity of bookishness, and only overcomes this handicap by reason of its deep moral earnestness. During these years he recognizes the value of the symbol as a means of heightening style and making it concrete, and comes to realize its spiritual character. His earlier admiration for the elegance or passion of oratory is gradually transformed into a devotion to simplicity. Berkeley, Bacon, Channing, Swedenborg, Plato, and Coleridge stimulate an innate dualism, and furnish or suggest major philosophic theorems, which in turn influence his conceptions of style. He is led to read books of science, and becomes acquisitive of the analogies between matter and spirit therein suggested. By this time transcendentalism, Montaigne, and an inborn independence begin their work, so that the years from 1830 to 1838 see many important consequences: the development and statement of all his fundamental tenets; the formulation of his purpose to write literature which is the grouping of momentary impressions and hence runs the risk of inconsecutiveness; and

[47] *Natural History of Intellect.*

[48] *Nature, etc.*

[49] *English Traits: Literature.*

[50] *Jour.* V, 22.

the growth, in theory and practice, of his conception of a living style. The beauties of Walden thrill him, and the thrill is communicated to his expression. Having gained concrete human experience from country friends and neighbors and from his home life, he converts the material from these sources—with the help of hints and theories drawn from Montaigne, Plato, and the Platonists—into spiritual symbol and illustration. And it is in this complex fashion that he attains the style which he perhaps might have attained anyway, through the maturing of native tastes—a style live, muscular, yet ideally suggestive.

BIBLIOGRAPHY

BIBLIOGRAPHY

A practically complete Emerson bibliography (to 1918) may be made by combining (1) *A Bibliography of Ralph Waldo Emerson*, compiled by G. W. Cooke, Boston, 1908; and (2) the bibliography compiled by H. R. Steeves for the chapter (VIII, Book II) on Emerson, in the *Cambridge History of American Literature*, v. 1, New York, 1917. To this should be added *Bibliographical notes on Emerson*, H. R. Steeves, in Modern Language Notes, November, 1917.

This book is primarily based on the material found in the following:

Emerson, Ralph Waldo. *Complete Works*, Centenary Edition, Boston, 1903-4. (The volumes of the works are referred to in the footnotes by their full titles with these exceptions: *Nature, Addresses and Lectures*, which is abbreviated to *Nature, etc.; Essays, First Series*, and *Essays, Second Series*, abbreviated to *Essays I* and *Essays II; Letters and Social Aims*, abbreviated to *Letters, etc.; Lectures and Biographical Sketches*, abbreviated to *Lectures, etc.*)

Journals of Ralph Waldo Emerson, Ed. by Edward Waldo Emerson and Waldo Emerson Forbes. Boston, 1909-1914. (This is referred to in the footnotes as *Jour.*)

Correspondence of Thomas Carlyle and Ralph Waldo Emerson. Ed. by C. E. Norton. 2 v. Boston, 1883. (This is referred to in the footnotes as *C. E. Corr. I and II.*)

J. E. Cabot. A Memoir of Ralph Waldo Emerson, 2 v. Boston, 1887. (This is referred to in the footnotes as *Memoir I and II.*)

Expression, by John Burroughs, published in the *Atlantic Monthly* for November, 1860, is a faithful reflection of Emerson's opinions on style. It lays stress on duality as the central principle of good writing, and on metaphor and compression as its offshoots. Burroughs wrote this not as imitation, but as an original essay. So thoroughly imbued was he with the Emersonian letter and spirit at the time—he was only 23—that the most expert judges were deceived, and unhesitatingly attributed the essay, which had appeared anonymously, to Emerson. Lowell, editor of the *Atlantic*, ransacked the *Dial* for the essay, thinking it must be an Emerson which some one was trying to pass off on him. Newspaper writers credited it to him; *Poole's Index* followed suit; A. S. Hill quoted a sentence from it in his Principles of Rhetoric with the same ascription. (See Bliss Perry: *Life of Walt Whitman* (p. 160); Clara Burrus: *Our Friend John Burroughs.*) The present writer, led astray by Hill, then by Poole, labored under the same delusion because of the likeness of style and the identity of idea. Emerson himself may have felt the consonance, for in his essay on *The Superlative* (*Lectures, etc.*) he apparently borrowed a metaphor from Burroughs. In *Expression* appears: "Saxon words form the nerve and sinew of the best writing of our day; while the Latin is the fat." In *The Superlative* "The positive is the sinew of speech; the superlative the fat." Or Burroughs may have heard some such expression from Emerson himself, though none such occurs elsewhere in the *Works* or *Journals*, and *The Superlative* is apparently a late essay. (Or similar ideas may have given rise to the same metaphor by both men, independently.)

The following is a selected bibliography of material, which, biographically, critically, or philosophically, seems of especial interest in connection with Emerson's style:

ALBEE, JOHN. *Remembrances of Emerson*. New York, 1901.

ALCOTT, AMOS BRONSON. *Concord Days*, Boston, 1872.

Ralph Waldo Emerson. Boston, 1888.

ARNOLD, MATTHEW. *Discourses in America*. London, 1885.

BABBITT, IRVING. *Masters of Modern French Criticism*. Boston, 1912.

BEERS, H. A. *The Connecticut Wits and other Essays*. New Haven, 1920.

Four Americans. New York, 1920.

BENTON, JOEL. *Emerson as a Poet.* New York, 1883.
BIRRELL, AUGUSTINE. *Obiter Dicta*, Second Series. London, 1887.
BLACKWOOD'S MAGAZINE. *The Habit of Emerson.* May, 1903.
BROWNELL, WILLIAM CRARY. *American Prose Masters.* New York, 1909.
BURROUGHS, JOHN. *Birds and Poets.* New York, 1877.
Emerson and the Superlative. Critic, Feb. 11, 1882.
Indoor Studies. Boston, 1889.
Literary Values. Boston, 1902.
BURTON, RICHARD. *Literary Leaders of America.* New York, 1904.
CARR, HENRY SNYDER. *Emerson as seen through his Prose.* New York, 1882.
CARY, ELIZABETH LUTHER. *Emerson: Poet and Thinker.* New York, 1904.
CHAPMAN, JOHN JAY. *Emerson and other Essays.* New York, 1898.
CLARK, J. SCOTT. *A Study of English Prose Writers.* New York, 1898.
COLLINS, JOHN CHURTON. *Posthumous Essays.* London, 1912.
CONWAY, MONCURE DANIEL. *Emerson at Home and Abroad.* Boston, 1882.
COOKE, GEORGE WILLIS. *Ralph Waldo Emerson: His Life, Writings, and Philosophy.* Boston, 1882.
COURTNEY, WILLIAM LEONARD. *Studies New and Old.* London, 1888.
CROTHERS, SAMUEL MCCHORD. *Ralph Waldo Emerson—How to Know Him.* Indianapolis, 1921.
CROZIER, J. B. *Key to Emerson. Fortnightly Review*, August, September, 1921.
CURTIS, G. W. *From the Easy Chair*, First Series. New York, 1893.
Other Essays from the Easy Chair. New York, 1893.
DAWSON, WILLIAM JAMES. *The Makers of English Prose.* London, 1906.
DUGARD, M. M. *Ralph Waldo Emerson, Sa Vie, Son Oeuvre.* Paris, 1907.
EMERSON, EDWARD WALDO. *Emerson in Concord.* Boston, 1889.
FIELDS, ANNIE ADAMS. *Mr. Emerson in the Lecture Room. Atlantic Monthly*, June, 1883.
FIRKINS, O. O. *Ralph Waldo Emerson.* Boston, 1915.
GARNETT, RICHARD. *Life of Ralph Waldo Emerson.* London, 1888.
Genius and Character of Emerson, ed. by F. B. SANBORN. Boston, 1885.
GUERNSEY, ALFRED HUDSON. *Ralph Waldo Emerson: Philosopher and Poet.* New York, 1881.
HARRIS, WILLIAM TORREY. *The Dialectic Unity in Emerson's Prose. Journal of Speculative Philosophy*, April, 1884.
HASKINS, DAVID GREENE. *Ralph Waldo Emerson.* Boston, 1887.
HIGGINSON, THOMAS WENTWORTH. *Contemporaries.* Boston, 1899.
HIRST, GEORGE C. *Emerson's Style in His Essays: A Defence. Harvard Monthly*, October, 1900.
HOLMES, OLIVER WENDELL. *Ralph Waldo Emerson.* Boston, 1885.
HUDSON, J. W. *The Religion of Emerson. Sewanee Review*, April, 1920.
HUNT, THEODORE WHITEFIELD. *Studies in Literature and Style.* New York, 1891.
IRELAND, ALEXANDER. *Ralph Waldo Emerson.* London, 1885.
JAMES, HENRY. *Partial Portraits.* London, 1888.
LOWELL, JAMES RUSSELL. *My Study Windows.* Boston, 1871.
MAETERLINCK, MAURICE. *On Emerson, and other essays*, tr. by M. J. Moses. New York, 1912.
MAULSBY, D. L. *The Contribution of Emerson to Literature.* Tufts College, 1911.
MOORE, CHARLES LEONARD. *A Master of Maxims. Dial*, May 1, 1903.
MORLEY, JOHN. *Critical Miscellanies*, v. 1. London, 1885.
MORE, PAUL ELMER. *Shelburne Essays*, First Series. New York, 1904.
Cambridge History of American Literature, v. 1. New York, 1917.
MOULTON, CHARLES WELLS. *The Library of Literary Criticism.* Buffalo, 1904.

PARKER, THEODORE. *Collected Works*, Centenary Edition. Boston, 1907.
PAYNE, WILLIAM MORTON. *Leading American Essayists*, 1910.
SANBORN, FRANKLIN BENJAMIN. *Ralph Waldo Emerson.* Boston, 1901.
The Personality of Emerson. Boston, 1903.
SANTAYANA, GEORGE. *American Prose*, Selections, etc. ed. by G. R. Carpenter. New York, 1900.
SCUDDER, HORACE E. *Men and Letters.* Boston, 1892.
SHERMAN, STUART PRATT, ed. *Essays and Poems of Emerson.* Introduction. New York, 1922. Reprinted in *Americans*, New York, 1922.
SLOAN, J. M. *Carlyle and Emerson. Living Age*, May 21, 1921.
SNIDER, DENTON J. *Biography of Ralph Waldo Emerson.* St. Louis, 1921.
SOCIAL CIRCLE IN CONCORD. *The Centenary of the Birth of Ralph Waldo Emerson*, 1903.
STEDMAN, EDMUND CLARENCE. *Poets of America.* Boston, 1885.
STEPHEN, LESLIE. *Studies of a Biographer.* Second Series, v. 4. London, 1902.
SUTCLIFFE, EMERSON GRANT. *Whitman, Emerson and the New Poetry. New Republic*, May 24, 1919.
WHIPPLE, EDWIN PERCY. *Recollections of Eminent Men.* Boston, 1887.
WOODBERRY, GEORGE EDWARD. *Ralph Waldo Emerson.* New York, 1907.
WOODBURY, CHARLES JOHNSON. *Talks with Ralph Waldo Emerson.* New York, 1890.

With relation to the influences, philosophical and literary, which were exerted on Emerson, I have found help in the following:

CARLYLE, THOMAS. *Works, Centenary Edition.* New York, 1898-1901.
COLERIDGE, SAMUEL TAYLOR. *Complete Works*, ed. by W. G. T. Shedd. New York, 1868.
FROTHINGHAM, OCTAVIUS BROOKS. *Transcendentalism in New England: A History.* New York, 1876.
GODDARD, HAROLD CLARKE. *Studies in New England Transcendentalism*, Columbia University, 1908.
Cambridge History of American Literature, Book II, viii. *Transcendentalism.* New York, 1917.
GRAY, H. D. *Emerson: a statement of New England transcendentalism as expressed in the philosophy of its chief exponent.* Leland Stanford Junior University, 1917.
HARRISON, JOHN S. *The Teachers of Emerson.* New York, 1910.
JEFFREY, FRANCIS. *Contributions to the Edinburgh Review*, v. 1. London, 1844.
MICHAUD, R. *Emerson's Transcendentalism. American Journal of Psychology*, January, 1919.
MONTAIGNE, MICHEL DE. *Essays*, tr. by Charles Cotton, ed. by W. C. Hazlitt. London, 1902.
PEABODY, ANDREW PRESTON. *Harvard Reminiscences.* Boston, 1888.
PLATO. *Dialogues*, tr. into English with analyses and introduction by B. Jowett, New York, 1871.
Princeton Review Theological Essays. New York, 1845-7.
REED, SAMPSON. *Observations on the Growth of the Mind.* Boston, 1826.
RILEY, WOODBRIDGE. *American Thought from Puritanism to Pragmatism.* New York, 1915.
Two Types of Transcendentalism in America. The Journal of Philosophy, May 23, 1918.
SCHINZ, A. *French Origins of American Transcendentalism. American Journal of Psychology*, January, 1918.
STAËL-HOLSTEIN, ANNE LOUISE GERMAINE (NECKER) BARONNE DE. *Oeuvres Completes;* publiées par son fils. v. 10, De L'Allemagne. Paris, 1820-1821.
WORDSWORTH, WILLIAM. *Prefaces and essays on poetry*, etc., ed. with notes by A. J. George. Boston, 1892.

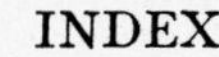

INDEX

INDEX